SPIRITUAL
VALUES
FOR EARTH
COMMUNITY

David G. Hallman

SPIRITUAL VALUES FOR EARTH COMMUNITY

Risk
BOOK SERIES

WCC Publications, Geneva

Cover design: Rob Lucas

ISBN 2-8254-1326-7

© 2000, WCC Publications, World Council of Churches
150 route de Ferney, P.O. Box 2100
1211 Geneva 2, Switzerland
Web site: http://www.wcc-coe.org

No. 89 in the Risk Book Series

Printed in Switzerland

Table of Contents

Preface

An invitation and a misunderstanding laid the basis for this book.

In 1997, I was invited by Prawate Khid Arn of the Christian Conference of Asia to give one of the theme addresses at an Inter-Religious Consultation on Climate Change being held in Kyoto, Japan, in December of that year in conjunction with the UN Climate Change Summit. Somehow, the theme he asked me to speak on got transformed in my mind into "Spiritual Values for Sustainable Living in the 21st Century". By the time I realized that I had focused on something other than what he had asked for, it was too late to change. After having presented the paper, I was encouraged by a number of people, including colleagues at the World Council of Churches, to consider expanding it into a book.

Whatever may have led me to misconstrue Prawate's original request, I found my perceived theme very enticing. I have worked on ecological issues for the United Church of Canada for almost 25 years and have been the coordinator of the World Council of Churches' Programme on Climate Change since 1995. While deeply engaged in education and advocacy work on ecological concerns, I have always been intrigued by the theological and ethical dimensions of these issues. I have sought in my earlier books to integrate those various dimensions,[1] but an explicit focus on spirituality was something new for me.

I have long been convinced that we who are active in advocacy work need to attend more specifically to the spiritual sources of our commitment, not only to ground the work firmly in our faith but also to benefit from the spiritual nourishment necessary for sustaining our energies over the long haul. I have also been aware of a broader constituency of people of faith who may not be actively engaged in issues of social or ecological justice but for whom spirituality concerns are central. Might it be possible to write something that would be helpful to them in making the connections?

Hence, *Spiritual Values for Earth Community*.

This is of course an enormous theme. But it seems to me that the issues facing our world are of such urgency that we must ask and struggle to find answers to the big questions. This book is intended as a small contribution to that. I hope it will be useful for individual reading and for group study.

In addition to thanking Prawate Khid Arn for the original invitation which led me to focus on the theme, I am indebted to various people for contributing to the writing through conversation, referring me to helpful material or providing feedback on drafts: Mark Burch, Nafisa Goga D'Souza, Bonnie Greene, Jean Olthius, Lillian Perigoe, Larry Rasmussen, Ernie Regehr, Martin Robra, Sandra Severs. Marlin Van Elderen of the WCC Publications office has been most helpful as I nursed the idea from concept to completion. My life partner Bill Conklin supported me in innumerable ways as I spent many hours of our collective time glued to my laptop computer.

Though I have tried to ensure the accuracy of all information included, errors may have crept in and I accept full responsibility if that is the case. While drawing on the work and insights of many colleagues in the ecumenical community, I am ultimately responsible for the analyses that form the basis of the book. Blame me not them if you find the arguments unconvincing.

Whether or not you agree with what I have written, I hope you will find it stimulating. The contribution of everyone is needed in the building of just and sustainable communities.

NOTE

[1] These include *Caring for Creation: A Canadian, Christian Response to the Environmental Crisis*, Winfield, Woodlake Books, 1989; *A Place in Creation: Ecological Visions in Science, Religion and Economics*, Toronto, United Church of Canada Publishing House, 1992; *Ecotheology: Voices from South and North*, Geneva, WCC, and Maryknoll, NY, Orbis Books, 1994.

1. Spiritual Values and Earth Community

Earth and its creatures are threatened.

The signs are everywhere: climate change, ozone-layer depletion, toxic and nuclear wastes, urban pollution, groundwater contamination, loss of agricultural land, diminishing fish stocks, unsustainable forestry practices. The list goes on. Add to that social and economic injustice, with the growing disparity between rich and poor, and one has a depressing picture of the health of human and natural communities.

These threats to the earth community come from many different sources – international trade agreements and economic policies, activities of transnational corporations, national industrial and agricultural practices, transportation systems dominated by the automobile, political and military conflicts, individual consumer decisions.

Such systems, institutions and behaviour are not immutable facts of nature. They have been created and are maintained by human decisions. As societies, we have chosen to organize ourselves in ways which are now producing destructive consequences for many people and many of the world's ecological systems. As individuals, we make countless daily decisions which add up to a life-style whose impacts on ourselves, our families, our neighbours, people around the world, future generations and the natural world are damaging.

Why do we as individuals and societies act in ways which have such disastrous consequences?

The argument of this book is that we make decisions as individuals and societies based on certain values. I contend that the dominant values influencing contemporary societies are:

- *human greed*, which is reflected in our patterns of materialistic consumption;
- the will for *domination*, which is manifested in the power of economic globalization; and
- *fear*, which gets expressed as violence.

These values are propelling us towards ever greater damage to the natural world and all that depends upon it, ourselves included.

But we do not have to stay on this destructive trajectory. Other values could form the basis of just and sustainable living patterns in the 21st century. I believe that there are potent spiritual values, expressed through – though not limited to – Christianity and other faiths, which could transform the way we live and organize our societies. The principal spiritual values I will highlight are gratitude, humility, sufficiency, justice, peace, love, faith and hope.

It is far from a simple task to substitute one set of values for another. Human behaviour and decision-making derive from many complex factors. In this introductory chapter, I want first to review some of the understandings over the ages of what determines human behaviour. Second, I will reflect on the place of values and specifically spiritual values in influencing behaviour. Third, I will look at concepts which have evolved over the past several decades in the effort to articulate what kind of societies are grounded in justice among peoples and respect for the broader creation. The evolution of those conceptual frameworks has led us to speak of "earth community".

Influences on human behaviour and decision-making

Much about what influences individual and collective behaviour is unclear. Social science research seems to indicate that we humans make choices and act out of complex motivations which include the basic survival instincts, but go well beyond these.

In order to understand better how values may influence individual and collective behaviour, we should perhaps go back several steps.[1] There is a long history of intellectual reflection about what determines actual human behaviour, but this question has been most explicitly addressed with the emergence of the disciplines of psychology and sociology. William James in 1887 published a series of articles which explored the role of instinct as the primary motivating factor in human behaviour. While some ancient and mediaeval writings focused on instinct, the major grounding for James's analysis came from the biological study of animals by 19th-century scientists such as Charles Darwin, combined with the emerging understandings of the human nervous system and basic organic reactions.

During the early part of the 20th century, however, instinct gradually lost favour among scientists because of its limitations in explaining more complex individual human behaviour and the collective behaviour of groups and societies. A range of other explanations were proposed including Freud's psychoanalytic theories, the behaviourist school of B.F. Skinner, and A.H. Maslow's hierarchy of needs moving through a spectrum from basic to more complex (physiological, safety, belongingness and love, esteem, self-actualization, cognitive and aesthetic). More recent studies of personality development have led many social scientists to conclude that the motivation for our behaviour is a complex interaction of factors, some of which are related to heredity and others to the environment in which we have grown and now function. The ultimate logic of these sciences would seem to imply that behaviour could be fully explained if we knew all the causal factors in one's personality development and if we knew all the circumstances in a situation of choice.

Supplementing these analyses of individual behaviour has been the contribution of sociology to our understanding of the individual within the context of the group and the organization and the behaviour of people as part of communities, institutions, societies and cultures. Sociologists speak, for example, of "norms" or "mores" as shared standards for behaviour in a society. Norms can evolve as a result of new developments or threats, and norms in one context can be in conflict with norms in another context. Insights from sociology can be helpful as we look in later sections of this book at how spiritual values can become more influential in determining the way we live our collective lives.

Other historical approaches to understanding and influencing human collective behaviour can be subsumed under classical political philosophy, more recent efforts to develop meaningful political theory and the realm of ideology. Ideologies in particular are action-oriented, often seeking massive changes in the existing situation in response to analyses of the problems with current conditions. Political theorists have identified various functions of ideologies, among them simplifying the view of the world, demanding action either for or against change and justifying the course of action taken. Liberalism, communism and fascism are perhaps the ideologies that come most quickly to mind, but much of this analytical framework of how ideologies function can be applied to the current dominance of the agenda of economic globalization with its emphasis on an unrestricted market and free trade.

Running parallel to and inter-related with analyses of the motivations of human behaviour is the history of philosophical and theological reflection on what human behaviour *should* be. Plato believed that a realm of pure ideas existed, of which life as we experience it is an incomplete imitation. Thus for Plato a moral life meant one in which a person tries to pattern his or her behaviour after such universal moral ideals as temperance, courage, prudence and justice. Aristotle reversed Plato's paradigm and suggested that ideas are a reflection of things. He began with life and tried to articulate the ultimate end or purpose of all things. For Aristotle the moral life was one that sought to bring about the full potential of one's true nature. Aristotle's philosophy laid the ground for more detailed examinations from an ethical perspective of actual human life and the social, economic and political institutions that humans create.

The inherent conflict between these contrasting understandings of the relationship between values and human behaviour still remains. I saw a young environmentalist recently wearing a T-shirt with the saying: "We may not be able to think ourselves into new ways of living but we can live ourselves into new ways of thinking." He was siding with Aristotle.

Over the centuries, many philosophers and theologians have deliberated on the nature of moral ideals and how they relate to our actual behaviour as humans. In the 1700s, Immanuel Kant maintained that it is only through "pure reason" that we can discern moral knowledge to apply in our lives. By contrast, David Hume argued that neither reason nor the knowledge we acquire by use of our reason can directly determine our behaviour. Rather, the principal motivating force for what we do is "passion", by which Hume meant emotions, attitudes, desires, wishes and needs.

A significant dimension in moral philosophy relevant to our discussion is the question of freedom of will. Regardless of the source by which we come to discern what is morally right, do we have unfettered freedom of will to choose one option over another? Theologies that assert that we have such freedom draw on a belief in the existence of God, who endows human beings with a spiritual dimension or soul, whose influence is not bound by physical, psychological or social factors. The soul can impel us to make choices based on higher and longer-term motivations. A non-religious variation of this bases its support for freedom of will on an analysis of the "moral self", the capacity of humans to make conscious choices based on principles of what is right even though such choices may seem to contradict what would be expected of such a person given their heredity and environment.

In modern and now post-modern times, we are witnessing a broadening of approaches to understanding the major influences on human behaviour. Male-dominated academic methodologies have been forcefully challenged by feminist thinkers, who have brought a sharp critique concerning how privilege that is structured into society on the basis of gender and class opens up opportunities for some and severely circumscribes opportunities for others. At a macro-economic level, ethicists and theologians from countries of the South have analyzed how privilege for some and oppression for the majority have become institutionalized within international economic relations.

Two other recent insights are worth noting. An understanding of the major influences on human behaviour and decision-making cannot emerge from a rational process alone, but must be open to appreciating insights derived from intuitive, emotional and spiritual sources. Again, it is feminist thinkers who have been most helpful in raising the profile of these other faculties. Second, we learn more about ourselves through an interactive process of engagement and reflection. Practical experience is indispensable for increasing our understanding. Intellectual analysis is impoverished without it.

This brief review of analyses of the sources of behaviour in psychology, sociology, political economy, philosophy and theology is not intended to come to a definitive conclusion. No one can fully explain why we act as we do as individuals and why we organize our societies as we do collectively. But it is apparent that the best minds over the millennia have struggled with this question, because it is an important one.

I have begun with this examination of theories of human behaviour because I expect that some readers may be inclined to dismiss the focus of this book on spiritual values as naive or idealistic, based on the assumption that identifying the relevant spiritual values will lead automatically to their implementation in practice at individual and collective levels. This assumption I do not make. I recognize the complexity of human behaviour, and I see spiritual values as fitting into a wider spectrum of influences on behaviour.

Given the diversity of explanations that have been offered regarding what determines human behaviour, I conclude that there is a variety of relevant factors, ranging from the micro dimension of neuro-physical response to specific stimuli of pain, through a wide matrix of hereditary and environmental aspects, to the macro dimension of choosing to abide by an abstract principle of what we discern to be morally correct. I see spiritual values as related to most of this continuum with the exception of the more reductionistic explanations. Throughout the book, I will try to illustrate how becoming aware of the operative current value systems can help us to see where and how they have an effect on human behaviour and, conversely, how we can use other more constructive values to help change individual and collective behaviour.

The nature of spiritual values

My hope for the future rests to a significant degree in my belief that there are spiritual values embedded in Christianity and other faiths that can help us live justly and sustainably if we can understand, rejoice in and live our individual and collective lives according to those values.

Though we talk rather glibly about values, it is more difficult to define exactly what they are. For example, how are values different from attitudes or beliefs?

For me, values refer to basic, foundational influences that affect how we think about and act towards ourselves and the world around us. Values can be positive or negative in influencing us towards life-enhancing or destructive choices. There is both a conscious and an unconscious dimension to our values. For instance, we can articulate what we believe to be our value system but our behaviour may show that we actually subscribe to a different set.

Values are more deep-seated and general than the attitudes we hold on particular subjects. Beliefs are conscious understandings to which we are committed and may well incorporate some of our values.

There is a close relationship between spiritual values and religious beliefs. When I talk about spiritual values, I am focusing on those creative, life-enhancing influences that are linked to our souls and our relationship to the spiritual dimension of existence. Spiritual values relate not only to our rational mind, but also to our heart, our emotions, our intuitions, our perceptions, our behaviour. Religious beliefs on the other hand are the way in which we describe the elements of our faith systems, usually through the use of sacred texts and traditions and commentaries on those sources. Though most religious beliefs are not verifiable in the scientific sense, they nonetheless do function primarily at a rational level in terms of our attempts to understand, articulate and communicate our faith. For me, spiritual values are more fundamental than religious beliefs, but that is not to assign them greater priority. Neither one is more important than the other; rather, they nurture each other.

In discerning the spiritual values from Christianity and other faiths which could undergird a more sustainable approach to social life in the 21st century, we find a significant resonance of ideas among the faiths in terms of the sacredness of the earth, the place of the human species as an integral member of the broader life-system, and the need to respect life including that which has gone before and that which will come after. There are certainly distinctions among the faiths in their understandings related to the natural world and our place within it, but the important commonalities provide a solid basis for interfaith collaboration in efforts to help reorient our societies towards greater social and ecological justice.

There are many people in our societies who look at religions with considerable cynicism. They point to the wars around the world where religion is a significant factor; the oppressiveness of various religions towards women, aboriginal peoples and minorities; and the undermining of concern about the well-being of the natural world as a function of teachings and practices of religions. A discussion about how spiritual values related to various faiths can support living for earth community needs to take seriously these contemporary critiques of religion.

Christians engaged in ecological issues are well aware of the accusation that certain elements of the Christian faith and tradition can be used, intentionally or unintentionally, to dissuade people from concern about and engagement in caring for the earth. There are many ways in which the Genesis reference to God's giving humans dominion over creation has been drawn upon to justify an exploitation of the earth's resources, with little concern for the ecological consequences. A focus on the importance of the next life has been used to minimize the need for concern about this life, and the emphasis on the superiority of humans as the only species with a soul has provided licence for disregarding the welfare of animals. The complexities of the Christian faith tradition in relation to earth community are certainly relevant to this discussion, but it is helpful to recognize that other faiths are not immune from certain paradoxes between their teachings and care for the earth. Take, for example, Buddhism, a faith that many would consider among the more ecologically benign.

Though different from Christianity in many ways, Buddhism shares some similar dynamics when it comes to concern about the well-being of creation. Both the teachings and practice of Buddhism encompass elements that would appear to place barriers to active engagement in caring for the earth and spiritual values that can help us grow in appreciation of our inter-relatedness with the rest of life.

For Western Christians, Zen Buddhism originating in Japan is probably the best known stream of Buddhism and here we immediately encounter complexities in relating Buddhist spiritual values to caring for the earth.

Zen Buddhism is focused on the practice of meditation whose aim is a journey of self-discovery. As Ruben Habito describes it,

> this tradition, which focuses on meditative practice, itself encourages the inward turn that enables the individual to disengage him- or herself from distracting and secondary "worldly" preoccupations and to focus on "the one thing necessary" – the awakening of one's true self, understood to be the basis of true inner peace and fulfilment.[2]

The pursuit of spiritual nourishment through Zen meditation, with its discipline on "listening within", can lead to a perceived separation of that which is interior from that which is exterior. There is an intentional spiritual withdrawing from the world outside in order to discover the self inside. This apparent split of the inner world and outer world – with the clear priority being concentrated on the inner – could diminish concern about the state of the earth on the part of Zen practitioners. There would be less spiritual rationale for being active in addressing pressing environmental concerns.

But just as deeper examination of Christian scripture and tradition has yielded new spiritual insights with profound ecological implications, so too more sensitive exploration in

Zen Buddhism leads to understandings that not only challenge those propensities to dismiss concern for the world but indeed illumine Buddhist spiritual values critical to saving the earth from human despoilment.

An examination of the practice of Zen Buddhism shows that there can be considerable application to ecological concerns. The three "fruits" of Zen practice are the deepening of one's mindfulness, the experience of awakening to one's true self, and the realization and personalization of this true self in one's ordinary life. The first fruit results in an integration of the various elements of one's life, so that the practitioner becomes acutely aware of the current moment and of being fully present in it. In the second fruit, where one recognizes one's true self, there comes a realization that there is no separation between one and the world, between subject and object. Thus the whole universe becomes one's concern. One comes to be able to see things from the perspective of other beings and thus to experience the interrelatedness of all things. The third fruit then leads one to apply these understandings to daily life. One is able to feel the suffering of the earth, which can then become a source of energy for transformation of how we live individually and collectively.

As important as interfaith efforts will be in the challenge of the global ecological crisis, we should not let the exploration of spiritual values in other faiths distract us from the primary task of delving into our own faith history, tradition and spirituality. Our aim is to address those negative values that have undermined sustainability, and to lift up those positive spiritual values that are critical for the long-term survival and flourishing of life on earth.

There are two risks in interfaith dialogue on the ecological crisis. One is that we will find it easier to focus on the gifts of another tradition than to come to terms with the problems and potentials in our own. Without the hard work of examining our own faith, especially for those of us within the Western Christian tradition, we will develop neither a comprehensive enough critique of the current situation nor a set of sufficiently alternative values for the future to make the kind of fundamental difference that is required.

The second risk is the temptation to appropriate spiritual ideas from other traditions at a superficial level. It would be an error to not take seriously enough the context out of which they have evolved and the many challenges that those communities face in the global context. For instance, it would be a disservice to First Nations (Indigenous or Aboriginal) Peoples to romanticize their spirituality about the earth without acknowledging the injustice, oppression and poverty to which many of them have been and continue to be subjected by the societies that have come to inhabit their land over the past centuries.

The concept of "earth community"

Half of the title of this book is "spiritual values". But to what end are we exploring spiritual values? For "earth community". For some, the term "earth community" will be new and it may seem almost as awkward as "just and sustainable living". Both of these phrases, which appear in the title and subtitle, are somewhat clumsy verbal attempts to capture a profound insight: the abundant life promised by Jesus and the shalom on earth towards which we are to work requires justice and respect towards the broader natural world. How can we articulate that integrated concept of social justice and ecological integrity? The ecumenical community has been trying for quite some time.[3]

More than a decade before the term "sustainable development" became popularized through the Brundtland Commission (World Commission on Environment and Development),[4] the concept of sustainability was being discussed at a WCC consultation of scientists, theologians and economists in Bucharest in 1974. We should not lose sight of the fact that the ecumenical community can claim some credit for conceptualizing sustainability.

The consultation in Bucharest was convened in response to the report *The Limits to Growth,*[5] in which an international group of scientists, economists and business and political leaders who formed the so-called Club of Rome sounded an alarm about how natural resource depletion, pollution and population growth were placing an intolerable strain on the earth's resources. What emerged out of the Bucharest discussion on the role of science and technology in the development of human societies was the articulation of a "concept called 'sustainability' – the idea that the world's future requires a vision of development that can be sustained in the long run, both environmentally and economically".[6] Charles Birch, an eminent biologist, was one of the speakers at the WCC assembly in Nairobi in 1975 and brought the Bucharest findings to the attention of the WCC. His eloquent promotion of the concept of sustainability was key in the WCC adopting a programme on "just, participatory and sustainable society" (JPSS).

The JPSS framework demonstrated the awareness of the need to link socio-economic justice and ecological sustainability. This has been a recurring theme within the ecumenical community and has been a gift to the broader global community. While many non-governmental organizations (NGOs), government departments, and international organizations have had either development concerns *or* environmental issues as their focus, the churches have tried to hold the two dimensions together. During the late 1970s, the WCC Department of Church and Society worked to promote the JPSS framework including at the 1979 conference on "Faith, Science and the Future"[7] in Boston at the Massachusetts Institute of Technology.

The just, participatory and sustainable society framework was expanded in 1983 at the Vancouver assembly of the WCC with the inauguration of the conciliar process on "justice, peace and integrity of creation" (JPIC). Some people feel that the JPIC focus lost some of the specificity of the JPSS framework since there no longer was explicit reference to "participatory" with its conceptual links to people's empowerment movements nor was "sustainable" any more in the title. The participatory theme could have been helpful now that an emphasis on communities has emerged as an important focus for the WCC. "Sustainable" may have clearer practical implications than "integrity of creation" which was a rather last-minute addition at the Vancouver assembly to a proposal which was originally referring only to justice and peace. On the other hand, others argue that JPIC makes an explicit reference to peace, which reminds us how destructive a force war and militarism is to both people and environment, and it adds a more specifically ecological and theological perspective with the concept of integrity of creation.

The important point is to recognize the conceptual inadequacy of any framework to describe sufficiently the breadth of our social and ecological concern. Such frameworks are constantly evolving in response both to how we understand our experiences and to new dynamics from the local to the global level.

Though the churches have done quite a good job in stressing the linkages among these various global problems, this is not to suggest that we have not had our share of debate within the ecumenical community about the relationship of socio-economic justice and ecological sustainability. The 1990 WCC world convocation on "Justice, Peace and Integrity of Creation" in Seoul and the lead-up to it stand out as a point in our history where this discussion was particularly vigorous. There were criticisms, mainly from persons involved in economic justice work, that the rising priority on environmental concerns was a Northern and largely middle-class diversion of the churches' attention from the more critical concerns of hunger, poverty and racial injustice.

The Seoul JPIC convocation did nonetheless take a significant step forward in the articulation of ten theological affirmations which, together with the analyses on which they are based, provide a clearer elaboration than we had had regarding, on the one hand, the inter-relatedness of economic inequity, militarism, ecological destruction and racial injustice and, on the other hand, the theological, ethical and spiritual basis for affirming and sustaining life in its fullness.[8] A further contribution of Seoul was to integrate these theological affirmations with more specific "covenants" in which the participating churches agreed to work together on programmes in justice, peace, integrity of creation and racial equity.

The United Nations Conference on Environment and Development (UNCED) held in Rio de Janeiro in June 1992 was a high point in ecumenical involvement in issues of sustainability and in interaction with the broader global community.[9] The ecumenical gathering in Rio was significant for a number of reasons. The WCC, along with representatives from other faith groups, helped to provide a substantial profile of religious communities at UNCED witnessing to our belief that the issues being addressed by the Rio Earth Summit had ethical, spiritual and theological dimensions which could not be ignored. Secondly, our time together as an ecumenical group laid the groundwork for network-building which resulted in further collaborative efforts later (e.g., a 1993 forestry consultation co-sponsored by Canadian and Philippine churches; WCC climate change work moving to a global level; initial conception of a theological resource which resulted in the WCC book *Ecotheology: Voices from South and North*[10]). Thirdly, the event diffused more broadly than ever before within the ecumenical community a recognition of the inter-relatedness of environment and development. We can point to a variety of evidence including increased programmes on environment and development within churches and new courses on ecotheology in seminaries in the North and the South.

On the other hand, the ecumenical gathering in Rio did not make a pivotal contribution to any new conceptualization of sustainability. More explicit work on this theme was done in 1993, when the WCC-related Visser 't Hooft organization sponsored a consultation entitled "Sustainable Growth: A Contradiction in Terms?"[11] A central focus of that consultation and the resulting booklet was the destructive and inequitable impact of the global economic system which emphasizes economic growth at all costs. The participants suggested that the term and concept of "sustainable development" was at risk of being eviscerated of its transformative potency by being expanded to include sustainable economic growth. In fact, this is precisely what we have seen in the documents that governments adopted at the Rio Earth Summit and most of the subsequent UN conferences.[12]

Much has happened to the concept of sustainability over the past twenty years and serious concerns can be raised about how its integrity is being compromised by current tendencies to misconstrue the term "sustainable development" to legitimize clearly unsustainable practices. "Sustainable community" is a term that we are now coming to use within ecumenical discussions related to the WCC's work on issues of economic justice and ecological integrity. While continuing to carry the long-term perspective of sustainability, it focuses on community in which the nurturing of just and equitable relationships both within the human family and also between humans and the rest of the ecological community can occur – in other words, justice within the whole of God's creation. Community can be understood at various levels, from the local context in which people spend their daily lives to the global human fellowship to the even more profound inter-relationship of all life on earth. Community is a useful focus also because it carries implications of relationships, responsibility and fulfilment.

"Earth community" moves us an important step further. It evokes an understanding of the wholeness and inter-relatedness of all life. Larry Rasmussen in his book *Earth Community, Earth Ethics* has made a major contribution in our ecumenical struggle to describe the vision towards which we feel called. Rasmussen illustrates how destructive are the basic conceptual frameworks of contemporary societies, which remain mired in assumptions that the human species is distinct from and superior to the rest of the natural world. Drawing on reflections of Czech President Vaclav Havel, Rasmussen observes:

> The world of "modern anthropocentrism" is deeply, even fatally flawed. The notions and institutions that issue from its ethics and spirituality, and depend upon them, must be set aside. A

16

moral universe limited to the human universe will not, under present circumstances, even understand life, much less serve it. Earth community requires a biocentric or a geocentric knowledge, ethic and faith.[13]

Rasmussen issues a profound challenge. Grounding our commitment to transformation in a vision of earth community compels us to recognize that (1) the survival of the human community is dependent upon a thriving natural world; (2) the forces of destruction and injustice within the human community are similar to those threatening the broader natural world; and (3) the long-term solutions lie in an integration of our struggles to bring about justice within the human community and sustainability of the global environment. Spiritual values are a key element in any transformation towards just and sustainable living, towards an understanding of the joy and responsibility of being members of earth community.

NOTES

[1] The following discussion about various schools of thought regarding determinants of human behaviour draws on analyses from a range of books including Elmer Sprague and Paul Taylor, eds, *Knowledge and Value*, New York, Harcourt Brace, 1967; Neil R. Carlson, *Psychology: The Science of Behavior,* Boston, Allyn and Bacon, 1984; Frederick E. Mosedale, ed., *Philosophy and Science: The Wide Range of Interaction*, Englewood Cliffs, NJ, Prentice-Hall, 1979; Judson R. Landis, *Sociology – Concepts and Characteristics,* Belmont, CA, Wadsworth Publishing, 1971; Richard Tarnas, *The Passion of the Western Mind,* New York, Harmony Books, 1991; Dieter Hessel, ed., *Theology for Earth Community,* Maryknoll, NY, Orbis Books, 1996.
[2] Ruben L.F. Habito, "Mountains and Rivers and the Great Earth: Zen and Ecology", in Mary Evelyn Tucker and Duncan Ryuken Williams, eds, *Buddhism and Ecology,* Harvard University Centre for the Study of World Religions, 1997, p.166.
[3] Some of the following material on ecumenical reflections regarding conceptual frameworks is drawn from an article I wrote for a WCC consultation on climate change and which was subsequently published in *The Ecumenical Review*, vol. 49, no. 2, April 1997, entitled "Ecumenical Responses to Climate Change: A Summary of the History and Dynamics of Ecumenical Involvement in the Issue of Climate Change".

[4] World Commission on Sustainable Development, *Our Common Future*, Oxford, Oxford UP, 1987.

[5] D. Meadows, et al., *The Limits to Growth: A Report for the Club of Rome*, New York, Universe Books, 1974.

[6] Wesley Granberg-Michaelson, "Creation in Ecumenical Thought", in David G. Hallman, ed., *Ecotheology – Voices from South and North*, Geneva, WCC Publications, 1994.

[7] See Paul Abrecht, ed., *Faith, Science and the Future*, Philadelphia, Fortress, 1979.

[8] World Council of Churches, *Now Is The Time: A Report from the Seoul World Convocation on Justice, Peace and Integrity of Creation*, Geneva, WCC Publications, 1990.

[9] World Council of Churches, *Searching for a New Heaven and a New Earth: An Ecumenical Response to UNCED*, Geneva, WCC Publications, 1992.

[10] David G. Hallman, *Ecotheology: Voices from South and North*, Geneva, WCC Publications, 1994.

[11] Visser 't Hooft Endowment Fund for Leadership Development, *Sustainable Growth – A Contradiction in Terms?*, Geneva, Visser 't Hooft Publications, 1993.

[12] David G. Hallman, "Creation and Justice in the World of Politics: The Ecumenical Community and the United Nations Challenge Each Other", a paper examining ecumenical involvement in the recent UN world conferences in Rio, Vienna, Cairo, Copenhagen and Beijing, prepared for a consultation of the World Alliance of Reformed Churches, April 1996 (available from the author).

[13] Larry Rasmussen, *Earth Community, Earth Ethics*, Marynoll, NY, Orbis, 1996, pp.17-18.

2. Values in Contemporary Western Societies

The values that we profess are not the values by which we live.

We may talk about justice, peace and ecological sustainability, but our individual life-styles and the economic realities of our Western societies seem to be based on a quite different set of values: consumerism, economic globalization, violence.

Many of us would protest that we are trying to live our lives as responsibly as possible; and making us feel guilty because of societal dynamics over which we have little influence is not going to help anything.

It is not that we intentionally are living greedy lives. Neither is it that we willingly subscribe to those globalization forces that are threatening the planet and increasing the gap between the rich and the poor. Rather, I believe this is one of the ways in which evil functions in today's world. Evil dulls our imagination and robs us of the creativity to envisage how life could be lived differently. At the individual level, we find it difficult to imagine being satisfied with any other way of life than surrounded with all the modern conveniences to which many of us in industrialized societies have become accustomed. At the societal level, we are told that there is no longer any other viable economic system than that which allows the market to function without restrictions and globalization and free trade to expand without impediment.

Three of the most potent forces determining the character of contemporary Western societies are consumerism, economic globalization and violence. Because of the dominance of Western culture through media and economic power, these three forces are also influencing other societies throughout the world. I venture to call them "values" on which Western societies are currently based. This may seem to be stretching our usual understanding of values as something positive and constructive. However, as mentioned in Chapter 1, I think of values as basic, foundational influences on our individual and collective behaviour. Values are not by my definition necessarily positive – they can be negative. The dominant influences in Western societies today are negative; they are destructive.

Consumerism

Consumerism has deeper historical roots and a more insidious grasp on Western cultures than we usually assume. We most often use the term to refer pejoratively to other people's compulsion to acquire material goods. Craig Gay's contribution in a recent collection of articles on *The Consuming Passion: Christianity and the Consumer Culture*[1] argues that consumerism is not some recent aberration in human behaviour but is a predictable consequence of the way in which Western cultures have developed since the Enlightenment. In rejecting the authoritarian control of religion and absolutist political powers, modernity has "liberated" people to define their own individual and collective identities and to pursue their own economic and social interests. Human happiness and fulfilment have increasingly been understood as attainable in the here and now through one's own endeavours. Paradoxically, there has been a continuous process of lowering our sights as to what constitutes fulfilment, from the more transcendent to the more mundane. Gay maintains that

> ... the essence of contemporary consumerism consists in two closely related commitments. The first is the commitment to self-creation and autonomous self-definition...; the second commitment entails shrinking the range of possible human aspirations to those circumscribed by secular experience.[2]

Already in the 19th century, Alexis de Tocqueville, in his analysis of American culture, perceived the growing influence of democracy, technology and scientific-rational explanations of life to shift the people's concentration away from the transcendent and from community into more individualistic and materialistic preoccupations:

> Most of the people in these (democratic) nations are extremely eager in the pursuit of immediate material pleasures... They think about nothing but ways of changing their lot and bettering it. For people in this frame of mind every

new way of getting wealth more quickly, every machine which lessens work, every means of diminishing the costs of production, every invention which makes pleasures easier or greater, seems the most magnificent accomplishment of the human mind.[3]

This lowering of our sights has reduced our capacity and interest in pursuing more profound levels of meaning in life. Various explanations have been offered for why and how this has happened. C.S. Lewis, among others, points to the power of science and technology to dominate nature, including human nature, as a key factor in the dissipation of the questing human spirit in favour of the more pedestrian pursuit of material comfort.[4] Søren Kierkegaard coined the term "philistine-bourgeois mentality" to describe the impact of modern consumer society in wasting away human imagination in the possibility of self and of God and replacing it with a fixation on comfort, safety and probability within a "certain trivial compendium of experiences".[5] Sociological, economic and political interpretations have also identified the role of advertising in creating the perception of need and the concentration of resources for scientific-technological research in the interests of commercial enterprise.

Craig Gay concludes that "so we have, since the 17th century and repeatedly thereafter, been encouraged to lower our sights philosophically and religiously for the sake of peace, prosperity, comfort and convenience".[6]

Though there may be historical roots to modern consumerism, the acceleration of the trend in recent times is so substantial as to be of almost a different quality. An article by David Myers in *The Consuming Passion: Christianity and the Consumer Culture* documents some of the increase of consumerist attitudes and practices based on a wide range of research:

- The UCLA/American Council on Education annual survey of nearly a quarter million entering collegians found that those agreeing that "a very important" reason for their going to college was "to make more money" rose from one in two in 1971 to nearly three in four in 1995.

- The same poll found that the proportion considering it "very important or essential" that they become "very well off financially" rose from 39 percent in 1990 to 74 percent in 1996; these proportions virtually flip-flopped with those considering it very important to "develop a meaningful philosophy of life". Materialism was up, spirituality down.
- An economist and two psychologists at Cornell have argued that economics professors are partly responsible for their students' materialism. Their national survey of college professors revealed that economists, despite having relatively high salaries, were more than twice as likely as those in other disciplines to contribute no money to private charities.[7]

Various measures demonstrate the great increase in consumption particularly since the second world war. The worldwide use of oil has increased from 436 million tons in 1950 to 3423 million tons in 1998, a jump of 2987 million tons or 685 percent over 48 years – an average annual growth of over 14 percent. Oil currently accounts for 30 percent of world energy use.[8] Automobiles have increased in number from 53 million in 1950 to 508 million in 1998. In relation to world population, this rise in the number of cars means that there is now one car for every 11.7 people, whereas in 1950 there was one car for every 49 people. Given the significant use of natural resources and energy needed to build cars and the polluting effect of cars in use, the explosion in automobiles worldwide has had a profound effect on the global environment. Air travel shows even more dramatic trends. World air travel rose 9260 percent from 1950 to 1998 in terms of passenger kilometres and 14,042 percent in terms of kilometres of freight transported. Aviation is the most polluting form of transportation per kilometre travelled.

The growth in consumption is reflected in carbon dioxide (CO_2) emissions from the burning of fossil fuels used in the production of electricity, many industrial and commercial processes, transportation and so on. CO_2 emissions have risen from 1609 million tons in 1950 to 6381 million tons in

1998, an increase of almost 300 percent. These emissions accumulate in the atmosphere and increase the concentration of CO_2. Since the industrial revolution, the concentration of CO_2 in the atmosphere has increased by about 30 percent, from 280 ppmv (parts per million by volume) around the year 1700 to over 360 ppmv today.[9] Over 80 percent of that increase has come from CO_2 emissions from the industrialized countries of the North. A broad scientific consensus now exists that this increased concentration of CO_2 in the atmosphere, accompanied by other human-produced greenhouse gases, is leading to a warming of the global atmosphere, which in turn is precipitating disastrous climatic changes.

There are many other serious environmental and social consequences of high consumption patterns including destructive impacts of various types of electricity generation (nuclear, fossil fuel, large-scale hydroelectric, etc.), massive landfill sites to deal with the huge quantities of garbage produced by our throw-away societies, and toxic waste sites often located close to poor or minority communities.

It would be somewhat easier to legitimize high consumption levels if such patterns were in fact improving the quality of life and bringing greater satisfaction and happiness to people's lives. Research on this subject is not encouraging.

It is clear that poverty creates a wide range of problems for people, including diminished health, high infant mortality, vulnerability to violence, and low satisfaction with one's circumstances. Increased economic and social well-being provides access to better food, shelter and educational opportunities. This inevitably entails some rise in consumption levels among the poor both in developing and industrialized countries.

However, once one has moved above a level at which basic needs are met satisfactorily, the correlation between increased consumption and improved sense of well-being is not nearly as significant. David Myers reports that

in the United States, Canada and Europe, the correlation between income and happiness is, as University of Michigan researcher Ronald Inglehart notes, "surprisingly weak (indeed, virtually negligible)". Happiness is lower among the very poor, but once a person is comfortable, more money provides diminishing return... The average American's disposable income (adjusted for inflation and tax changes) has doubled since the late 1950s. But happiness has not risen... Since 1957, the number telling the University of Chicago's National Opinion Research Centre that they are "very happy" has declined from 35 percent to 30 percent. People are twice as rich and a little less happy.[10]

Consumerism is exacting an intolerable environmental cost on the earth. It is a factor in the increasing gap between the rich and the poor. Even for those with the financial resources to indulge in unfettered consumer purchasing, it is not bringing them the satisfaction which they expected. As a dominant value in contemporary Western societies and with attempts to emulate it worldwide, consumerism is undermining the health of earth community.

Globalization

Economic globalization is in many ways an extension of consumerism to a worldwide level, posing significant threats to ecological sustainability and social justice. Globalization is an ambiguous term. As we try to describe it more specifically what we mean, we recognize that there are aspects of globalization that we would want to affirm. Surely it is a good thing that churches and other groups working to overcome injustice around the world can have increased contact to share resources, learn from each other and develop coordinated strategies through organizations such as the World Council of Churches and technologies such as e-mail and the Internet. Environmental problems such as the depletion of the ozone layer and climate change are global by definition, and hence it is vital that the whole world work together to try and solve them. Such cooperative efforts are made possible through global organizations such as the United Nations, scientific and environmental bodies, non-governmental organizations and the like.

However, aspects of globalization concerning which there are many reasons to be justifiably disturbed include economic domination of the many by the few, an ideology of free markets and trade liberalization in order to increase production and consumption, the power and lack of accountability of transnational corporations, and cultural homogenization through American merchandizing and media. I will refer to these dimensions as "economic globalization", to help delineate the destructive aspects of globalization that represent a real threat to the building of just and sustainable communities.

As we move into the 21st century, economic globalization demonstrates some of the same dynamics as colonialism and imperialism did in earlier centuries. There is an evangelical-istic zeal among its proponents that reflects a belief in the superiority of the model of free markets, trade liberalization and minimal regulation for corporations. Decisions are made in a few power centres with the consequences felt by people around the world who have no input. Whole countries and indeed regions are discounted and made vulnerable to the needs and choices of those exercising economic leverage. Fortunately, as with community and nationally based revolts against colonizers, we also see the development of movements of resistance which are challenging the social and environmental destructiveness of economic globalization.

Economic globalization represents for its supporters a positive, almost spiritual, value on which a world economy should be refashioned and to which national and local economies should be subject. These advocates argue that not only will economic globalization increase wealth but that it is necessary in order to solve major problems such as poverty and environmental threats. They maintain that growth in the global economy will inevitably benefit national economies, allowing governments to meet the social needs of their people and have the resources necessary to pay for environmental solutions.

This is the all-boats-will-rise-with-the-rising-tide argument, a somewhat dated and ironic image in these days of concern about rising sea levels resulting from climate change. It is not a new argument and neither are the responses to it. Herman Daly is one of the few progressive economists who has been critiquing traditional approaches and proposing more ecologically sustainable and socially just models. Daly describes what he calls a "catechism of growth fallacies" in which most mainstream economists ignore the social and environmental consequences of economic systems which emphasize constant growth in production and consumption.[11] Daly and John Cobb, Jr, who together wrote the book *For the Common Good: Redirecting the Economy Toward Community, the Environment and a Sustainable Future*, make a convincing case that "further growth beyond the present scale is overwhelmingly likely to increase costs more rapidly than it increases benefits, thus ushering in a new era of 'uneconomic growth' that impoverishes rather than enriches".[12] Such warnings have largely been ignored as many of the more powerful governments and businesses pursue dreams of unlimited growth through globalization.

The expanding biotechnology industry is a good example of how economic globalization is functioning in today's world. A tremendous amount of research is under way, primarily within industrialized countries, focused on developing genetically modified organisms (GMOs). The intent of most of this agriculture-related research is to employ GMOs to increase crop yields or milk production and to create food products that will be more durable and resist various forms of pests and growing stresses. The biotechnology industry has started encountering resistance to their products from consumers because of concerns about the long-term safety and health of the products. Alarm bells are also being sounded related to the effects of biotechnology on the environment and the impact on the livelihoods of farmers. These concerns have been much more prevalent in Europe and some of the developing countries than in North America, where public awareness of genetic engineering has emerged more recently.

In part because of the growing concerns, the biotech industry has been promoting the new technologies as a key to solving the problem of hunger in the developing world. They argue that seeds can be genetically modified to tolerate drought and other environmental stresses better and to be resistant to various pests, thus reducing the need for using harmful pesticides. Who could object to these seemingly laudable benefits of spreading Western technology around the globe? Yet objections are coming from unexpected sources – the farmers who are the intended users of the seeds, for one.

Farmers and environmental groups in India, Brazil and various other countries of the economic South contend that the promotion of the biotechnology industry has much more to do with increasing corporate profits than with relieving hunger. A classic example presented as evidence is the so-called "terminator seed" technology. In order to ensure continued income, the agribusiness companies that are promoting biotechnology insist that farmers purchase new seeds from them for each growing season. In some places, companies are using legal means to try to prohibit farmers from using seed produced by one season's crops for planting for the next year. An ingenious approach developed initially by US-based Monsanto has been to modify seeds genetically so that the crop they yield will not produce seeds that can be used by the farmers for the next season, hence, the label "terminator seeds".

The most vocal objections to this new form of indenture have been raised by farmers in India, who say that it will increase their costs substantially and undermine traditional sustainable farming approaches. Vandana Shiva and her colleagues in India and the United Kingdom development organization Christian Aid have documented a significant increase in suicides among farmers unable to cope with the financial stress and loss of independence attributable to the control exerted by the large agribusiness companies and their new biotechnologies.[13]

Though biotechnology is one of the newest areas of scientific and commercial innovation, many of the dynamics of this form of modern globalization are similar to those in

colonial times. The power rests primarily with the industrialized nations and their corporations, whereas the developing
countries and their peoples are vulnerable subjects of
exploitation. Regardless of the arguments put forward by the
companies, the benefits of this biotech revolution in the agricultural systems will accrue mainly to the corporations, and
the social and environmental costs will be experienced by the
farmers and communities in the developing countries.

Concentration of power in the hands of a relatively small
number of industrialized countries and corporations based
mainly in the North is one of the characteristics of contemporary economic globalization. Combined with the heavy
debt loads of many developing countries and the so-called
Structural Adjustment Programmes imposed on their
economies by international financial institutions, this concentration of power reduces many governments' capacity to
meet their people's social needs and to protect the environment. In addition, international currency speculation, which
can produce huge windfalls for the speculators but creates no
real benefit in terms of increased employment for people,
further undermines countries' sovereignty by making their
currencies and interest rates vulnerable to wide fluctuations.
This is not just a matter of macro economics but affects bil-
lions of ordinary people worrying about how they will pay
for bread and milk.

The ideology of the market within the context of economic globalization relies heavily on the continuing expansion of free trade and investment. One of the shifts of power
that is most threatening to sustainable communities is the
ceding of significant economic authority by governments
from their democratically elected parliaments to the largely
unaccountable World Trade Organization. In addition, the
WTO and economic ministries in many industrialized
nations appear determined to ensure that trade and investment agreements take precedence over environment and
social treaties negotiated through the UN. Such a hierarchy
could severely impede attempts to address climate change
and other earth community issues. The WCC and other non-

governmental organizations hope that recent intergovern-
mental negotiations related to climate change will lead to
policies aimed at reducing global use of fossil fuels, the
burning of which is the major source of the emissions leading to a warming of the global atmosphere. But if economic
agreements are given priority over environmental treaties,
then domestic policies to address such issues as climate
change could be ruled as unfair restrictions to free trade and
investment and thus disallowed.

It is likely that developing countries would be disadvan-
taged the most by WTO rules. Several other international
processes could compound this vulnerability, including the
inadequate responses to the need for debt relief, the "Comprehensive Development Framework" through which the
World Bank intends to coordinate and control almost all
development aid, and the new international financial archi-
tecture project of the International Monetary Fund (IMF).
The already powerful industrialized nations and transnational corporations are intent on solidifying their influence
over the direction of economic globalization for their own
benefit. There are precious few indications of any awareness
or concern with how such approaches to globalization
impede the creation of socially just and ecologically sustainable communities throughout the world.

One of the reports adopted by the WCC eighth assembly
in Harare in 1998 summarized the impact of economic globalization and its challenge to the churches:

> Globalization is not simply an economic issue. It is a cultural,
> political, ethical and ecological issue... The vision behind glob-
> alization includes a competing vision to the Christian commit-
> ment to the oikoumene, the unity of humankind and the whole
> inhabited earth... The logic of globalization needs to be chal-
> lenged by an alternative way of life of community in diversity...[14]

Violence
Violence is the third operative value in contemporary
society we must address. It may seem strange to refer to violence as a value. But looking at societies around the world to

discern the fundamental influences on their development, one sees violence emerging again and again in different forms. Certainly, one can argue that violence is a consequence of such factors as social disintegration, conflicts over scarce ecological resources, economic inequality, ethnic rivalries and military aggression. But I believe that violence is more than just an effect. In subtle and insidious ways, contemporary societies have come to structure violence into their policies and practices as an instrument to maintain privilege and control. Violence is an explicit and implicit value related to militarism, ethnic rivalry, economic domination, social conflict and environmental destruction.

War is the most blatant example of violence. During the 20th century, we witnessed the slaughter of millions of people during armed conflicts. Civilian fatalities, both inadvertent and intentional, vastly outnumbered soldiers slain in battle. Whole communities were destroyed and indeed attempts were made to annihilate entire peoples. Military activity devastated vast ecosystems, with consequences for both people and many other species.

The 20th century saw an evolution of war from the large interstate conflicts of the two major world wars to smaller, more regionally based conflicts within countries. Rivalries between ethnic, religious and political groups played a major role, with almost unbelievable savagery in such countries as Cambodia, Guatemala, Rwanda, Bosnia, Ireland, Sudan and Kosovo. There also were wars that were quite clearly initiated to protect economic interests. Though the rich countries involved in the 1991 Gulf war argued that their intention was to thwart the aggression of Iraq upon Kuwait, it is difficult not to conclude that the principal concern was the protection of the oil interests of their transnational corporations in the Middle East.

The insidious violence that forms a foundation of much of the global and national economic policies is much less visible than war or the threat of war. Yet, as we have said, rich industrialized nations and their transnational corporations are intent on solidifying their power through a range of international economic organizations and agreements related primarily to trade and investment. Economic systems and policies are structured so as to protect the privilege and wealth of the already powerful, even if it means the victimization of local communities, farmers, marginalized peoples and ecosystems. The WCC's Programme to Overcome Violence describes this dynamic:

> Violence originates in part from systems and structures that rob people of the opportunity for humáne living conditions which help sustain their lives. One such system is globalization, the transnationalization of capital and production based on a single, worldwide logic of exchange. Globalization increasingly centralizes control and power, removing decisions about fundamental matters of economic, social and political life from the local and national level to the global level. This system also imposes on individuals and societies worldwide norms of economic growth, consumerism, privatization, individualism, and the presumption of winners and losers. These norms, accompanied by such remote control, accentuate and accelerate human fragmentation, isolation, and exclusion for the profit of the few, contributing significantly to violence among individuals, groups and nations.[15]

The natural world is a particularly vulnerable victim of the violence perpetrated by economic systems. Human societies have viewed mineral deposits, forests, water systems and animal life primarily as "natural resources" for exploitation. It is ethically justifiable when use of the natural world is made in order to meet basic survival and quality of life needs. It is quite another thing when such exploitation explodes in relation to the carrying capacity of the earth to meet the luxury demands of societies gone wild with consumerism and economic globalization.

Economic systems are also often a factor in violence that forms the basis of social relationships. Inner-city conflict between gangs and the violence associated with robbery and drugs most frequently occur within poor and minority communities where educational and employment opportunities are the most neglected. During the latter decades of the 20th

century, many industrialized countries enacted policies to
reduce national deficits and revised tax laws to provide
greater privilege to wealthy individuals and to corporations.
A major consequence has been the reduction of social programmes and the increase in the gap of wealth and opportunity between the rich and the poor in these Northern societies. The dynamic has been even more pronounced in countries of the South where governments have been forced by
Structural Adjustment Programmes demanded by the International Monetary Fund to cut back in public spending
including for social, health and educational supports.
Hunger, disease and the disintegration of communities are
forms of violence against people when caused by economic
policies which deprive people of basic necessities of life.

In addition, violence within families often has economic
connections. With deregulation and the pressure to become
more competitive, many companies have made dramatic cuts
in their work-forces. The cut in family income for those who
find themselves unemployed increases the stress already
present in modern societies. There is a high correlation
between economic stress and spousal and child abuse.

The protection of environmental resources by the rich for
the rich is another form of violence against people who are
denied access to those resources. Israel hoards water for such
things as wealthy citizens' swimming pools while Palestini-
ans badly need it for their basic needs. Peasants in Central
and South America have been driven off land or denied
access to it by rich landowners who raise cattle to export
meat to Northern countries. Aboriginal peoples in Canada,
the United States, Mexico, Australia and Aotearoa New
Zealand have struggled for generations to retain or regain
access to lands and resources which supported their communities before being deprived of them with the arrival of Euro-
peans.

In its various manifestations, violence is endemic in
contemporary societies as a means used by the powerful to
protect their wealth and privilege. The pursuit of just and
sustainable communities is not possible without societal

32

transformation in which peace with justice replaces violence as a foundational value.

NOTES

[1] Rodney Clapp, ed., *The Consuming Passion: Christianity and the Consumer Culture*, Downers Grove, IL, Inter-Varsity Press, 1998.
[2] Craig Gay, "Sensualists without Heart: Contemporary Consumerism in Light of the Modern Project", in Clapp, *The Consuming Passion*, p.20.
[3] Alexis de Tocqueville, *Democracy in America*, trans. George Lawrence, Garden City, NY, Doubleday/Anchor, 1969, p.462.
[4] See C.S. Lewis, *The Abolition of Man*, Glasgow, Collins, repr. 1978.
[5] Søren Kierkegaard, *The Sickness unto Death: A Christian Psychological Exposition for Upbuilding and Awakening*, trans. Howard V. and Edna H. Hong, Princeton, NJ, Princeton UP, 1980, p.41.
[6] Gay, "Sensualists without Heart", p.33.
[7] David Myers, "Money and Misery", in Clapp, *The Consuming Passion*, pp.52-53.
[8] Most statistics in this section are drawn from Lester Brown et al., *Vital Signs 1999*, Worldwatch Institute, New York, W.W. Norton, 1999.
[9] John Houghton, *Global Warming: The Complete Briefing*, Cambridge, UK, Cambridge UP, 1997, p.24.
[10] David Myers, "Money and Misery", in Clapp, *The Consuming Passion*, pp.55,59,60.
[11] For a discussion of these economic arguments and counter-arguments, see the chapter on "Economics: From Exploitation to Sustainability", in my book *A Place in Creation: Ecological Visions in Science, Religion and Economics*, Toronto, United Church of Canada Publishing House, 1992.
[12] Herman Daly and John Cobb, Jr, *For the Common Good: Redirecting the Economy toward Community, the Environment and a Sustainable Future*, Boston, Beacon Press, 1989, p.2.
[13] See *Selling Suicide: Farming, False Promises and Genetic Engineering in Developing Countries*, London, Christian Aid, 1999.
[14] Diane Kessler, ed., *Together on the Way*, report of the WCC's eighth assembly, Harare, Zimbabwe, December 1998, Geneva, WCC Publications, 1999, pp.254,258.
[15] World Council of Churches, "Programme to Overcome Violence: Assumptions and Principles", Geneva, WCC Commission on the Churches on International Affairs, 1994.

3. Spiritual Values for Justice and Sustainability

In Chapter 1, we looked at the nature of spiritual values, their relationship to other individual and collective dynamics that influence our choices and actions, and what we mean by earth community as a vision of the type of societies towards which we should be striving. Chapter 2 focused on an analysis of contemporary societies and the dominant, operative values that influence them – consumerism, economic globalization and violence.

This third chapter forms the heart of the book. In it we will reflect upon a number of spiritual values that could make a profound difference to our world if we were able to integrate them as foundational influences in our individual and collective lifestyles. Organizing our lives and our societies on the basis of such values would increase the social justice of our communities and the health of our relationship with the broader world.

The spiritual values I have chosen are gratitude, humility, sufficiency, justice, love, peace, faith and hope. Two comments need to be made about this selection. First, there may be other important values not included. These are my priorities, but in no way do I want to minimize others. I welcome contributions that add to or challenge my analysis. Second, these spiritual values are not distinct one from the other but very interconnected. Discussing each one in turn may seem somewhat arbitrary at times, but once seen together they will make a comprehensive whole.

A colleague from India, Nafisa Goga D'Souza, on reading a draft of this book, questioned whether my list of spiritual values – chosen from the context in which I write – would be the ones identified by the tribal, poor and marginalized peoples with whom she works. She conjectured that these peoples would more likely place values such as solidarity and empowerment at the top of the list. I acknowledge that my choices are shaped by my growing up and living in a Western industrialized culture. Nafisa poses a provocative challenge, one which I hope will be reflected in the discussions that this book precipitates.

We do not change our individual and collective behaviours just by articulating a set of abstract spiritual values nor by trying to will ourselves into observing them. Behaviour and social transformation come about by an interaction of ideas, values, experience and reflection. The lived experience of our current life-styles and of experiments with alternate approaches is critical to any process of change. Hence, with each spiritual value that I discuss in this chapter, I include a brief case study of just and sustainable living. The examples I have chosen relate to a variety of our chosen values, not just the one in the section in which they are placed. Some of the case studies are ones that relate directly to individual choices; others describe initiatives at a more global level. They are intended to demonstrate that we can indeed change the way we live and the manner in which we organize our societies through a combination of spiritual values, new ideas and collective action. Though the case studies described are exciting, in their current and potential impact they are still relatively modest. But they are a beginning, perhaps leading to other creative initiatives until, collectively, they will add up to a more profound impact.

That is how I believe the Spirit of God works – not by a single massive, centralized, dominating action but rather by a vast multiplicity of small initiatives often in unexpected places. I understand the nature of the Spirit as anarchic – dynamic, creative, uncontrollable, a vast number of sparks igniting new life in many different places.

1. Gratitude

Rejoice always, pray without ceasing, give thanks in all circumstances; for this is the will of God in Christ Jesus for you. (1 Thess. 5:16-18)

Many people in contemporary Western societies seem chronically dissatisfied. Complaining has become a high art. People are unhappy about their lives, their governments, their social institutions, their churches. Even though they live in the wealthiest societies in history, people manifest constant dissatisfaction with their material well-being. "I'm depressed – I think I'll go shopping" is a commonly heard comment, spoken only half in jest.

Consumerism is both the result of a profound spiritual emptiness and a source contributing to that very same emptiness. People feel a lack of meaning and purpose in their lives and seek to fill the void with materialism and modern entertainments, especially television. It costs a lot of money to buy these products and services, putting ever-increasing pressure on people to work harder and earn more money. That leaves less time for the more significant sources of spiritual fulfilment to be found in nurturing relationships with family, friends, the natural world and God. Thus the pursuit of material gain reinforces the spiritual vacuum that plagues so many people in contemporary Western societies.

Why do we appear unable to make the connection and focus our energies on cultivating those nurturing sources of satisfaction rather than pursuing the illusory panaceas of material consumption? It is by now a cliché to blame the advertising profession for "manufacturing needs" in people's minds, and to point to industry in general for building in obsolescence so people are forced to replace last year's model with this year's version. That is certainly part of the answer, but only part.

The negative cycle of spiritual emptiness feeding a mania for consumption which in turn leads to more spiritual poverty is not going to be broken unless we are able to interject a radical alternative. This leads me to the first of the spiritual values that I would propose for living sustainably in the 21st century: gratitude.

The verse from Thessalonians 5 is for me one of the most challenging in the Bible. How can we be expected to give thanksgiving in all circumstances when there is so much suffering, poverty and ecological destruction in the world?

Indeed, when I delivered the paper that was the origin of this book at the Inter-Religious Consultation on Climate Change and Sustainability during the Kyoto Climate Summit in December 1997, the initial reaction of some of the Christian participants working with the poor in India and Bangladesh was one of incredulity that I would cite gratitude as the first spiritual value. The people with whom they worked are struggling for justice and could hardly be expected to give thanks for the poverty in which they are mired. My initial response was twofold. I reminded them, first, of the *context* of my analysis, as a person coming from a relatively affluent Western country directing my critique primarily to that society, and second, of the *content* of my analysis: that I was recommending gratitude for the life-enhancing gifts of God, not one's materialistic well-being or lack thereof.

My response however was eclipsed by another from a Hindu contributor from India who reflected that, indeed, gratitude needs to be a fundamental spiritual value at work in everyone's life regardless of their economic or social status. Without a profound gratitude for life and its blessings, no matter how meagre they may seem, one's spirit can easily dissipate in a cycle of depression, anger, frustration. She argued that a spiritual life founded on gratitude was necessary for maintaining the physical and emotional resources required for the long struggle for justice.

Though most of us in the more affluent societies are not facing the threats to basic survival experienced by so many in countries such as India and Bangladesh, we nonetheless could also ask how it is possible to "give thanks in all circumstances" when faced with illness, economic stress, family breakdowns, violence. The response of the Indian participant in Kyoto is instructive to us as well. Life is always filled with challenges, which can overwhelm us unless we have a dynamic and well-grounded spiritual reservoir on which to draw. Gratitude and thankfulness to God for the blessings of life are among the most important foundations for that reservoir.

Psalm 67 offers an example of the inter-relationship of God's generosity and justice and our gratitude:

> May God be gracious to us and bless us
> and make his face shine upon us,
> that your way may be known upon the earth,
> your saving power among all nations.
> Let the peoples praise you, O God;
> let all the peoples praise you.

Let the nations be glad and sing for joy,
    for you judge the peoples with equity
and guide the nations upon the earth.
Let the peoples praise you, O God;
let all the peoples praise you.
The earth has yielded its increase;
    God, our God, has blessed us;
May God continue to bless us;
    let all the ends of the earth revere him.

According to the Psalmist here, we have been blessed in multiple ways through God's saving power, justice, guidance and with the bounty of the earth. Not only have we experienced God's graciousness in the past but we are assured of its continuance in the future. In response, the Psalmist calls us and all peoples to praise God and to do so with joy and exuberant thanksgiving. Psalm 67 concludes with an appeal that God grant us blessing so that all the earth may worship God with respect, gratitude and devotion. God's blessing is not portrayed as contingent on our being grateful but in response to such generosity; no other response is conceivable but praise and thanksgiving.

The concept of gratitude expands with a marvellous explosion of praise in Psalm 148. Not only are we as human beings to praise God, but all the rest of creation is to give thanks as well: the sun and moon, the shining stars, the water-spouts and ocean depths, fire and hail, snow and ice, mountains and hills, fruit trees and cedars, wild beasts and cattle, creeping things and winged birds. Stars and birds giving praise? The image seems preposterous to the rationalistic Western mind. But the scriptures point here to a profound ecological insight which will recur repeatedly in our examination of spiritual values from not only the Christian tradition but other faiths as well. All that exists is inter-related, both in the web of life and through a relationship to the source of creation. We human beings are part of that creation, but only part. We share much more in common with other species than we usually assume.

38

But even if we can stretch our minds to incorporate the broader network of life in our concept of an integrated creation, how can we conceive of other elements giving praise, of being thankful to God? To ask the question is to illustrate our limited imaginations. It is not only by verbalizations through human language that praise can be given. In the Genesis 1 creation story, God repeatedly affirms that what has been created is good. Those elements in turn reflect the glory of God and give praise to God through their very being.

For what reason is everything to give praise? For the miracle of being created is the Psalmist's response:

> Let them all praise the name of the Lord,
> for he spoke the word and they were created (Ps. 148:5).

The very fact of existence is the rationale for thanksgiving.

Gratitude infuses dark moments in the Bible as well. During the last supper, Jesus took the bread and wine and, after blessing them and giving thanks to God, distributed them to his disciples, admonishing them never to eat or drink such again without remembering the sacrifice which he was about to make. In Christian liturgy for 2000 years, thanksgiving for these basic elements of earth's bounty has been interwoven with gratitude for the greatest gift of all. It is not by accident that we refer to the ritual as "celebrating" the eucharist.

The New Testament letter to the Colossians brings together important elements for our understanding of the ecological implications of spiritual values. Colossians 1:15-20 is a wonderful hymn of praise, focusing on Christ as the source of all creation and agent for all reconciliation:

> In him everything in heaven and on earth was created...; the whole universe was created through him and for him...Through him God chose to reconcile the whole universe to himself, making peace through the shedding of his blood upon the cross – to reconcile all things, whether on earth or in heaven, through him alone (Col.1:15,20).

Near the end of Colossians, the author depicts the spiritual garments that most appropriately suit followers of Jesus:

> ... compassion, humility, gentleness, patience...; to crown all,
> there must be love, to bind all together and complete the
> whole... Be filled with gratitude..., sing thankfully in your
> hearts to God, with psalms and hymns and spiritual songs...
> (Col. 3:12-16).

Viewed together, these verses invoke an image of a total
creation inter-related through the creative and reconciling
power of God in Jesus, in response to which we are to live
our lives based on peaceful values, including gratitude.

Other faiths have their own approaches to depicting the
wonder of creation before which we ought to stand in awe
and gratitude. Ranchor Prime tells a story drawn from the
Hindu tradition about a cobbler and his conversation with
Narada, the great teacher and messenger of the god Vishnu.
The cobbler lived under a great banyan tree that was so huge,
with so many smaller trunks hanging down from the
branches, that it was like a small forest. One day he was visited by Narada, who said that Vishnu had sent him to the cobbler to answer any question that he might have. The cobbler,
flustered that he should be granted such a privilege, could
only think of a simple question to ask: "What was Vishnu
doing when you saw him?" Vishnu, who wanted to teach
Narada a lesson, had anticipated that this would be the cobbler's question and had told Narada to reply that Vishnu was
threading an elephant through the eye of a needle. Though
surprised by the answer, the cobbler responded, "Well, only
Vishnu could do that!" Narada was bemused by the simple
man's faith. He had not expected him really to believe that
Vishnu was threading the elephant and chided him gently on
his innocence. But the cobbler replied:

> "Why can't Vishnu do that? Nothing's impossible for Vishnu.
> This world is full of his miracles. He makes the sun rise each
> day. He makes the wind blow. He makes the rivers run and the
> trees and flowers grow.
>
> "Look at this," the cobbler went on as he bent to the ground
> and picked up a seed from beneath the banyan tree. "Inside this
> seed is a banyan tree as big as the one above us. It's just wait-
> ing to come out. If Vishnu can squeeze a whole banyan tree into

such a tiny seed, surely he can thread an elephant through the eye of a needle!"[1]

Though science can now explain the biological process by which a seed evolves into a tree, it cannot capture the mystery of creation as well as this Hindu story. The simple cobbler appreciated the beauty of creation and the generosity of Vishnu. The great Narada recognized the cobbler's wisdom in seeing the hand of Vishnu in everything and felt chastised for taking such magnificence for granted.

Expressions of gratitude for creation within various faith traditions are often linked to profound understandings of the interconnectedness of all life and our human dependency on other elements within ecological systems. The Kayapó Indians from the rainforests in the Amazonian heartlands of Brazil had many oral hymns of praise. Of the few which have been recorded, there is a deceptively simple one in praise of the little red ant:

> The trails of the fire ant *(mrum-kamrek-ti)* are long.
> They are ferocious *(akrê)* like men.

> But the little red ant of our fields *(mrum-re)*
> is gentle like women;
> They are not aggressive *(wajobôre)*.
> Their trails meander like the bean vines on the maize.

> The little red ant is the relative/friend of the manioc.
> This is why women use the little red ant
> to mix with urucú
> to paint their faces in the maize festival.

> The little red ant is the guardian of our fields
> and is our relative/friend.[2]

The seeming simplicity of this song belies the ecological wisdom it incorporates. The red ant is connected in an interdependent relationship with the manioc plants whose roots are a critical food source to the semi-nomadic Kayapó. The Indians are thus reliant on this little creature, the red ant. Over the past few decades, biologists have become more aware of a dynamic in ecosystems which they have called cooperative evolution or co-evolution. The domesticated manioc plant used by the Kayapó is an example of co-evolution in its relationship to the red ant. The manioc both nurtures and benefits from the activities of the little red ant. Modern biologists confirm that this reciprocal relationship between the manioc and the little red ant has conferred mutual evolutionary blessings on each.

The recognition that the ant and the manioc are connected as "relative/friend" is echoed in the last line with the little red ant being acknowledged as the "relative/friend" of the Kayapó. The song is evidence of the Kayapó's awareness of this interdependency. Their response is one of gratitude and appreciation, illustrated in concrete expressions such as the paint made from the ants as adornment for the women's faces during the harvest celebration.

Gratitude as a spritual value is present throughout the sacred texts and traditions of many faiths. When we give thanks, we are recognizing our dependence upon God, other people and the sources of life around us. Gratitude forces us to relinquish control, the assumption that we alone are responsible for our well-being. The Kayapó Indians recognize this in the song of the little red ant, and Hindus are reminded of it in the cobbler's story. The Psalmist celebrates the name of the Lord who spoke the word and all were created, and the apostle Paul rejoices that in Jesus Christ everything in heaven and on earth was created. Rabbi Abraham Heschel wrote that humankind "will not die for lack of information but it may perish for lack of appreciation".[3] A beautiful image-filled Jewish prayer of gratitude reads:

> Even if our mouths were as full of song as the sea,
> > and our lips as full of praise as the breadths of heaven,
> > and our eyes as bright as the sun,
> > and our hands as outstretched as the eagles of the sky,
> > and our feet as swift as gazelles,
> We could not thank you enough.[4]

How can we grow in gratitude? Spiritual discipline through a regular daily pattern of prayer and thanksgiving is one effective tool. Pausing to say grace before meals forces us to take a breath and acknowledge that the nourishment of which we are about to partake is the product of more than our hands. Grace before meals is also a witness to others who might be around our table that Christian faith is an important dimension of our lives and at least places in their minds the idea of the appropriateness of giving thanks to God.

Prayers of thanksgiving help us focus intentionally on what is most important to us. In the depth of prayer, we are less likely to thank God for the latest shopping bargain than we are for a new birth, recovery of health, a reconciled relationship, the joy of time spent in communion with nature. The discipline of prayer can make us more conscious of the priorities that we truly value. It is as if in our talking to God in a spiritual mode, God opens our rational minds to new insights.

Being aware of what is of greatest value in terms of our relationships with God, family, friends, the global community and nature is a necessary but not sufficient step in living lives that reflect gratitude as a fundamental principle. We need a spiritual discipline, not only to regularize our prayer life but also for our everyday decision-making. Our decisions about life-style, work schedules, use of time and money should be guided by our perception of what is most valuable in life as perceived through our prayer life. Our resources can then be channelled towards the support and enhancement of those relationships. Spiritual discipline is an appropriate term in this context because it takes effort not to succumb to the mind-numbing propaganda of our contemporary consumer advertising and materialistic culture. We have to make conscious assessments in our daily lives about what actions would be life-enhancing and what would carry destructive consequences for the spiritual or physical well-being of those around us, including the natural world.

It is more challenging to imagine how we can incorporate gratitude more explicitly into our collective lives. There are several risks in assessing the many blessings for which we should be thankful as a society. Those who have leadership responsibility could use the process to legitimize their current practices and undermine opposition to change intended to improve social equity and ecological integrity. Also, giving thanks for our societal blessings can lead to a comparative assessment with other societies resulting in arrogance and pride. Finally, as a product of the preceding two concerns, celebrating our collective blessings could be distorted theologically as an affirmation that God has chosen and blessed our community above all others.

However, a serious effort to identify and give thanks for the blessings we enjoy collectively can, if we are conscious of these risks, be a radical process. It need not just be focused on what is but on what could be and should be. The aspects of life together in society that people most value have largely to do with supports within family, community and state that allow for health, security and happiness. These might include access to nutritional food, affordable health care, freedom from violence and the opportunity for meaningful employment. Civil society[5] is probably best positioned to facilitate such an assessment because it does not have vested interests in maintaining the status quo and can help organize people for action towards attaining those benefits.

Gratitude also propels us towards a response of caring. When we are grateful for something, we inevitably grow in our concern for it. If we are grateful for the natural world, then we begin to care about its health. We need greater resources to support long-term action to protect the environment than a sense of guilt or obligation. Thankfulness for the beauty, mystery and pragmatic importance to our own lives of healthy ecosystems gives a positive force to our motivation.

A case study: Forest Stewardship Council

Trees and forests figure as important members of creation in the sacred texts of various faiths. Larry Rasmussen describes how trees have served for millennia as "religious symbols of a sturdy, renewed and upright way of life. Trees speak and tell stories, stories of life, resistance, death and new life."[6] He cities examples from different faiths:

- The Hebrew Bible begins with the tree of life *(etz chaim)*, set in the midst of the Eden of origins (Gen. 2:9).
- The Christian Bible, which also begins in Eden, ends with the tree of life as well, this time not in the garden of origins but in the city of destiny: New Jerusalem (Rev. 22:1-2).
- In East Africa, sacred trees are the meeting place with a powerful spirit and often the place of important community decisions.
- The Iroquois Confederacy (an American Indigenous People) pictures planet earth held together with the gently encompassing roots of the tree of life. Without this tree, things fall apart.
- For Buddhists, the Bodhi Tree is fixed at the world's axis *(axis mundi)*, and in its shelter Prince Siddhārta attained enlightenment as the Buddha.[7]

The biological and ecological sciences have documented the critical role that trees play in supporting life on earth. They function to sustain local ecosystems, preserve water resources, provide habitat for other species, occupy a key place in the atmospheric mixture of oxygen and carbon dioxide, and offer humans a wealth of gifts for nourishment and shelter.

Yet forests are under threat from human activity in most regions of the world, jeopardizing the life of many other species and undermining important life-sustaining processes for our species as well. How can we translate gratitude as a spiritual value into practical action which can help protect forests? Supporting the Forest Stewardship Council is one such option.

The churches in Canada were one of the early members of the Forest Stewardship Council (FSC). Through the Taskforce on the Churches and Corporate Responsibility, the Canadian churches had worked to influence the land management practices of forestry companies in Canada. This ecumenical coalition developed a model code of practice for forest land management and pressured companies through shareholder resolutions to adopt such a code and report annually on their performance.

When the FSC was formed, the Canadian churches supported it because they saw it as an innovative mechanism to help transform forestry practices around the world to become more sustainable and respectful of the communities affected by the industry's activities, in particular aboriginal communities.

The Forest Stewardship Council was founded in 1993 as an international non-profit organization to support environmentally appropriate, socially beneficial and economically viable management of the world's forests.[8] Its international headquarters are in Oaxaca, Mexico. The FSC is an association of members consisting of diverse group of representatives from environmental and social groups, the timber trade and the forestry profession, Indigenous Peoples' organizations, community forestry groups and forest-product certification organizations from around the world. The FSC recognizes that there is huge public concern about the destruction of the world's forests. More and more people demand products that come from well-managed forests. This demand has led to many different labels on forest products, making claims such as "for every tree felled at least two are planted". Many of these claims are irrelevant or misleading. An authoritative study by the Worldwide Fund for Nature (WWF) found that of a sample of eighty different environmental claims found on wood and paper products, only three could even be partially substantiated. FSC aims to clear up the confusion by providing a truly independent, international and credible labelling scheme on timber and timber products. This will provide the consumer with a guarantee that the product has come from a forest that has been evaluated and certified as being managed according to agreed social, economic and environmental standards.

The FSC has developed a set of internationally recognized principles and criteria of forest stewardship on the basis of which national and local standards are then prepared by FSC-related committees in those respective areas. There is then a process of accreditation carried out by certification bodies functioning under rigorous procedures and standards set out by the FSC. Certified forests are visited on a regular basis to ensure that they continue to comply with the principles and criteria. Products originating from forests certified by FSC-accredited certification bodies are eligible to carry the FSC logo, if the chain-of-custody (tracking the timber from the forest to the shop) has been checked.

On the day I was writing this section, in August 1999, an article appeared in the morning paper reporting a significant breakthrough for the Forest Stewardship Council:

> Home Depot Inc., the largest US home improvement retailer, will stop selling wood from environmentally endangered areas, a move that one environmental group said was a "great victory for the forests".
>
> The chain that claims it sells more lumber than any other single company in the world, announced yesterday that the phase-out of so-called "old growth" wood will take effect in 2002. In addition to cutting out sales of lumber from threatened forests, Home Depot said the action also would cover the whole range of wood products from brooms to doors...
>
> In addition, the company said that it is moving towards selling only wood that has been certified "responsible growth", by the Mexico-based Forest Stewardship Council. Only 1 percent of wood currently available is certified by the group as meeting environmental, social and economic standards.[9]

By purchasing products that carry the FSC logo, we can support good forest stewardship and provide an incentive to other organizations to improve their management. If one cannot find the FSC logo on products, one should ask stores to stock them. The more customers who request products from well-managed forests, the greater is the incentive for forest owners to provide them. In this way, individuals, companies and organizations such as churches can exert a direct and positive influence to improve stewardship of the world's forests.

NOTES

[1] Ranchor Prime, "Introduction: The Banyan Seed", in *Hinduism and Ecology: Seeds of Truth*, London, Cassell, 1992, p.3.
[2] Peter Knudtson and David Suzuki, *Wisdom of the Elders*, Toronto, Stoddart, 1992, pp.52-53.

[3] Abraham Heschel, *Who Is Man?*, Stanford, CA, Stanford UP, 1965, p.83.

[4] Cited in video *Keeping the Earth: Religious and Scientific Perspectives on the Environment*, 1996, Union of Concerned Scientists, Two Brattle Square, Cambridge, MA, USA 02238-9105.

[5] "Civil society" is a term that has come into increasing use referring to the social sector beyond government and business. Civil society encompasses voluntary organizations; women's groups; children and youth, environmental and social organizations; labour; and in some contexts, educational systems. In many countries, particularly throughout the regions of the economic South, civil society acts as the primary impetus for social change aimed at improving the economic and social well-being of the people and the protection of the environment.

[6] Larry Rasmussen, *Earth Community, Earth Ethics*, Maryknoll, NY, Orbis Books, 1996, p.196.

[7] *Ibid.*, pp.196-98.

[8] For more details, see the web page for the Forest Stewardship Council, from which some of this information is drawn: www.fscoax.org

[9] "Home Depot shuns old-growth timber as firm goes green", *The Globe & Mail*, Toronto, Canada, 27 August 1999.

2. Humility

An argument arose among them as to which one of them was the greatest. But Jesus, aware of their inner thoughts, took a little child and put it by his side, and said to them, "Whoever welcomes this child in my name welcomes me, and whoever welcomes me welcomes the one who sent me; for the least among all of you is the greatest" (Luke 9:46-48).

Humility is a second essential spiritual value for earth community in the 21st century.

Jesus was forever confounding people's assumptions about status. Even the disciples, who had such a close relationship with Jesus during his ministry, lost sight of his message about humility and fell prey to the sin of pride, arguing over who was the greatest among them. Though the gospels do not record their reaction, Jesus' use of a little child must have been a sobering chastisement for the disciples. In the social order of those days, children were quite inconsequential. Jesus identifies himself with the child, and says that he is welcomed by those who extend their hand not to the powerful ruler, the influential merchant or even the high priest, but to a child. Greatness does not subsist in the trappings or privileges that society values but in the meekness of a little child.

The 20th century could be characterized by the absence of humility among the human species. Overweening pride was the order of the day and the destructive consequences fill the history of the age.

Politically, we saw the rise of nationalisms and ideologies based on beliefs of ethnic or social superiority. The bloodiest wars in human history were a direct result. Struggles for dominance between superpowers with different economic systems brought the world to the brink of nuclear war. The perceived triumph of free-market capitalism exacerbated a trend towards economic globalization dictated by a few power centres in industrialized countries and proselytizing a Western cultural model.

An explosion of technological innovation opened vast new possibilities for improvements in human welfare. Unfortunately, the benefits accrued primarily to the already privileged in the world. Some developments had widespread applicability, such as enhancements in public health and education. However, the majority of technological advances were related to an industrialization model focused on an unremitting expansion in production and consumption. With the gap between the rich and the poor continuing to grow, vast numbers of people were unable to afford the new products and services. Moreover, the dominating industrialization and agricultural models required massive inputs of natural and artificial resources and resulted in far more wastes being pumped into soil, water and air than the ecosystems could absorb.

Technological innovation raises difficult philosophical and pragmatic questions about human initiative. Just because we *can* do something, does that mean we *should*? Are there justifiable criteria for restricting research and development? Who should have the right and responsibility for making such decisions? Do proposals for assessing and limiting development not smack of the centralized control-style economies that have proved to be so disastrous?

Biotechnology is one current area in which ethical judgments are having to be made about the appropriateness of certain types of research and the application of scientific knowledge. There may be the potential for significant improvement in people's health and quality of life through the use of some new processes developed in this burgeoning field. On the other hand, many unanswered questions exist about the longer-term consequences for people, other species and the environment.

While not wanting to oversimplify issues about the reach of human initiative, I would contend that one of the underlying dimensions is the spiritual struggle between human pride and humility.

Traditional interpretations of Judaeo-Christian scriptures have contributed to a perception of the human species as the pinnacle of creation. Several critical verses in the first chapter of Genesis seem to present a picture of humans being given unlimited authority over all other creatures. In particular, we read in Genesis 1:26-28:

> Then God said, "Let us make humankind in our image, according to our likeness; and let them have dominion over the fish of the sea, and over the birds of the air, and over the cattle, and over all the wild animals of the earth, and over every creeping thing that creeps upon the earth."

Cursory readings of other Bible verses compare humans and other creatures and appear to indicate that God assigns greater value to our species. Those references have been used and misused to provide theological endorsement of a paradigm which places all of the rest of creation under the power and control of human beings. God is assumed to have created all the rest of creation for the sole purpose of human use.

In one of my earlier books entitled *A Place in Creation: Ecological Visions in Science, Religion and Economics*,[1] I analyzed the relationship between, on the one hand, this theological understanding of God giving humans authority over

all and, on the other hand, the development of the technological capacity to manipulate nature through the Western
scientific and industrial revolutions. There have been some
fascinating interconnections among the disciplines of science, religion and economics over the years that have contributed to one of the major sources of the current ecological
crisis. I am referring to the paradigm that we humans are better than the rest of nature and that the natural world only has
purpose in so far as it can be used to contribute to so-called
human progress.

But this is not just an interesting intellectual development. The perception of humans as being divinely ordained
to exploit the natural world for our own ends has had profound negative consequences on the well-being of the environment. These consequences have in turn had a destructive
impact on the health of many species including our own.

Some leading historians and environmentalists, most
notably the American Lynn White, Jr,[2] have accused the
Judaeo-Christian tradition of being a major source of the ecological crisis because of the part it has played in fostering this
image of humans as legitimate exploiters of the rest of creation. There are many in our secular world who still hold this
negative view of Judaeo-Christian heritage. However, over
the past 25 years, theologians have embarked on a quite
remarkable and exciting reanalysis our scriptures and traditions and have rediscovered quite a different understanding
of what God's intention may be for how we humans relate to
the rest of the created order.

One of the first major steps in this transformation away
from what we might call "dominion theology" was stewardship theology. Stewardship theology argues that the unique
role of humans within the created order is not to be understood as a position of unfettered authority but rather as one
of caring responsibility. In his book *The Steward: A Biblical
Image Come of Age*,[3] Canadian theologian Douglas John
Hall studies the references to the steward in both the Old Testament and in Jesus' parables in the New Testament, and then
draws analogies to our relationship to the natural world.

Based on his analysis of the role of the steward in looking after the household on behalf of the master, Hall argues that we do not own the earth, just as the steward does not own the household. It belongs to the master. We are to care for it with the same loving concern with which the master would and we will be held responsible for our actions and punished if we abuse the occupants of the household.

Stewardship theology provided a major shift in our understanding of how we are to relate to the natural world. It struck a blow at excessive human pride and made us recognize, with humility, that we have responsibilities towards, not unlimited rights over, the earth. But stewardship approaches still assume that we humans have a good understanding of how that responsibility should be exercised. A more benevolent gardener image has replaced the exploiter image, but the stewardship approaches of the gardener still evoke a management model.

More recent theological developments have pushed us significantly further in acknowledging that we must approach the natural world with much greater humility. Feminist theology and the spiritual traditions of Indigenous Peoples recognize the inherent non-rational wisdom present in much of the natural world. Ecological systems function in ways that use only as much resource as can be replenished and dispense only as much waste as can be recycled into the system. Recent discoveries in biology have found that there are more cooperative relationships within the natural world than had earlier been assumed when the competitive survival of the fittest paradigm was the dominant scientific model.

Eco-feminist theology uses a very different image to describe the place of humanity. Rather than the pyramid of the dominion theology with humans at the top and the rest of creation below, eco-feminist theologians describe the "web of life" in which all parts are inter-related. Rosemary Radford Ruether has spoken of inverting the hierarchy based on a criteria of what is indispensable for the survival of life.

> In a system of interdependence, no part is intrinsically "higher" or "lower". Plants are not "lower" than humans because they don't think or move. Rather, their photosynthesis is the vital process that underlies the very existence of the animal and human world. We could not exist without them, whereas they could exist very well without us. Who, then, is more "important"?[4]

This ecological perspective challenges our current human arrogance about our place in the natural world.

The spiritual traditions of Indigenous Peoples also provide an alternate and more humbling way of looking at our relationship with the rest of creation than the usual Western approach of dominance. Stan MacKay, a Cree who was the first Native person elected as moderator of the United Church of Canada, has said that

> indigenous spirituality around the world is centred on the notion of relationship to the whole creation. We call the earth our mother and the animals are our brothers and sisters. Those parts of creation which biologists describe as inanimate we call our relations. This naming of creation into our family is an imagery of substance, but it is more than that, because it describes a relationship of love and faithfulness between human beings and the creation.[5]

With such a powerful indigenous image of all creation as an inter-related family, we move further away from the notion that the natural world has value only in its use and exploitation by the human species. With humility, we begin to view the world with affection and respect. Living justly and sustainably in the 21st century will require this kind of humbler understanding of our relationship to nature as being part of the web of life or the family of creation.

Christianity is not alone in having had a largely anthropocentric view of the world. Islam, arising out of some of the same cultures and utilizing some of the same sacred texts as Judaism and Christianity, has generally assigned humans an exalted status. To date, there appears to be only a limited reassessment of that perspective within Islam. However, Muslim scholars who are concerned about ecological issues are reminding their people of neglected passages of the Quran and teachings of the holy prophet Muhammad which draw a less strict line of division between humans and the rest of creation. Al-Hafiz B.A. Masri points out that the Quran and Hadith emphasize that animals share a lot in common with people – they belong to communities and are loved and created by God:[6]

> There is not an animal on earth, nor a bird that flies on its wings, but they are communities like you... (Quran 6:38).
> All creatures are like a family *(ayal)* of God: and he loves the most those who are the most beneficent to his family *(Shu'ab al-Iman)*.

Assuming a humbler self-understanding in relation to the rest of creation may be an important step for us humans in moving towards more just and sustainable living, but the spiritual value of humility also raises other problems for us in contemporary societies. Again, scripture is simultaneously a source of new insights and new complexities. Humility, as an indispensable foundation for Christian life, is a truth that God wishes to impress upon us through Jesus, in whom God "emptied himself, taking the nature of a slave..., humbled himself, becoming obedient to death, even to death on a cross" (Phil. 2:7-8). Christ's teaching confirmed this and he calls on us to live in a similar way when he says, "Learn from me for I am meek and humble of heart" (Matt. 11:29).

These images and words of Jesus are likely to make us uncomfortable in this age of individual and collective self-assertion. There would certainly be a legitimate discomfort among women, racial and sexual minorities and others who have been victimized by a dominating white patriarchal culture. Do such minorities not need precisely to be assertive and proud of their own identities? Is it not our ethical responsibility to stand up against authoritarian structures and individuals and challenge systems which exploit others in the human and non-human community? There is a parallel here to the reaction which I alluded to earlier of Asian anti-poverty workers at the gatherings in Kyoto, who found an emphasis on gratitude incomprehensible for their work among the most marginalized in their societies.

I do not want to minimize the difficulties here. Humility is one of the most challenging spiritual values for us to comprehend, appreciate and implement in our age. But it is essential. Only with an acceptance of our limitations and our dependence on other beings (human, non-human and spiritual) can we hope to develop communities characterized by social and ecological sustainability. But how can we reconcile this with our desire not to be the victims and pawns of oppressive forces intent on accumulating the maximum possible wealth and power?

Fortunately, the options are not mutually exclusive. Jesus' life and teachings as well as other scriptural sources provide essential clues for our understanding of humility as in fact a potent spiritual and political power. Humility is often misunderstood to imply something weak or spineless. It does not. The practice of humility requires great strength and courage. Humility bridles the tendency to estimate and evaluate ourselves as greater than we are. This is the vice of pride, which is the root of much sin and is in fact the path to considerable weakness and failure because the challenges of life are always going to be greater than our own individual resources. Humility on the other hand, rooted in justice and truth, keeps us mindful of our total dependence on God and God's creation. With that broader appreciation of the resources accessible to us and with cooperative methodologies for building relationships and sustainable communities, we are much stronger than when we operate with exaggerated confidence in our individual strength.

How can humility be translated into practical strategies for sustainability in our individual and collective life-styles? Fortunately, we are not bereft of models. There are historical and contemporary examples from which we can glean key elements of what it would mean to live with humility as a guiding spiritual value. Hildegard of Bingen, Gandhi, Mother Teresa and Jean Vanier are models. One of the signs of humility in each of these people is that their energy has not been directed towards their own well-being. Rather they have been intensely concerned with the welfare of others both human and non-human. Second, from their writings and recorded comments, we can surmise that they have had a profound relationship with God or what they understood to be the spiritual dimension of creation. This relationship nurtured their soul. They recognized that their strength came not from their own resources and they acknowledged their dependence on the source of life. Their spiritual lives were not self-absorbing but led them beyond themselves. Third, their humility was not manifested exclusively in their own individual life-style. They were all keenly aware of injustice in the world and dedicated their lives to challenging it and seeking to bring about change. Often this meant a profound respect for and solidarity with the most marginalized in the society of the day.

Canadian Jean Vanier is the founder of the L'Arche communities, in which persons with disabilities live together with others who wish to share their lives. Vanier writes in his book *Becoming Human*[7] that "it is the weak and those who have been excluded from society who have been my teachers". Kenneth Bagnell has commented in a review on Vanier's book, in the context of the contemporary resurgence in spirituality.

> There is a crucial question about the interest in spirituality: Has it any social conviction? Does it lead us to be our brother's keeper? Or is it so centred on the self that it's just another form of selfishness, one more way we enhance ourselves while blithely overlooking or smoothly rationalizing the pain of others? In the view of one of the most spiritual men of our time, Canadian Jean Vanier, the best way to prevent this perversion is to deepen spiritual life by relating to other people – the forgotten, the neglected. In this way, we may minimize self-indulgence but also learn what is at the heart of the true spiritual life: to love when it's not easy to love, to forgive when it's not easy to forgive.[8]

Humility as a spiritual value at the individual level calls us to recognize our dependence on God, on the natural world and on others and to live lives that respect those others, both human and non-human. Furthermore, we are not just called to avoid harming others in the earth community, but rather actively to seek their well-being. In the story of Jesus admonishing the disciples about their arguments on greatness, he does not just insist that they acknowledge or tolerate the little child. He says that they are to welcome the child. Both the Old and New Testaments count the refusal to offer hospitality as a much more serious sin than we assume in our day. True hospitality means opening one's home and sharing one's resources with those in need – and doing it with joy. As individuals, we are given such opportunities daily in a myriad of simple and challenging ways, everything from feeding the birds to taking in refugees.

Translating humility into public policy would similarly focus resources on those most in need. A major priority would be to adopt economic and political decisions which have as their goal the protection and sustenance of the biosphere. This would invert the traditional egotistical assumption that humans are the most important elements of creation and all else is accessible for exploitation for our own purposes. Rather, humility would propel us to acknowledge our dependence on the ongoing processes of creation and to act in ways that protect them both for our own sake and for theirs.

A case study: Bench Marks – principles for global corporate responsibility

It is one thing for us to assume responsibility ourselves for relating to other people and the broader creation with greater humility and hospitality, quite another to require it of those with significant political or economic power. But churches in the United Kingdom, Canada and the United States are seeking to do just that with respect to transnational corporations (TNCs).

The Bench Marks project is intended to force corporations to be more accountable for the impact of their policies and activities on the human and natural communities where they operate, and through such accountability to become more responsible. One can see such efforts as thematically in line with Jesus' discussion about greatness. In our world, transnational corporations have tremendous power. Yet, Jesus says that such greatness is not greatness in his eyes. Rather, it is the least among us – the most vulnerable – who is the greatest. The church coalitions involved in the Bench Marks project have dared to take Jesus' ethics to heart and to demand of mighty corporations that they become accountable for the actions that cause harm to vulnerable communities.

Churches are not alone in putting pressure on corporations. Many non-governmental organizations, both in countries of the economic South as well as in industrialized Northern nations, are active in researching the growing influence of transnational corporations and developing strategies focused on specific destructive policies and practices.

The United Nations has also made efforts to require greater corporate responsibility, but its failure provides a lesson in the close interconnection between economic and political power. The UN had a body called the UN Centre for Transnational Corporations which conducted various studies about the social and environmental impact of companies. In 1992, the UN Centre submitted to one of the preparatory meetings for the Rio Earth Summit a list of principles for minimizing the negative impact of TNCs on environment and development. The governments of industrialized countries involved in negotiating the draft agreements for the Earth Summit refused to let the principles go forward because of industry pressure. The attempts of the UN Centre to prepare even a voluntary code of conduct for TNCs continued to be vigorously opposed by business after the Earth Summit, and eventually the whole effort died. The UN Centre has since been restructured out of existence. According to one former staffer of the UN Centre:

> The heart of the issue is that multinationals fear even the semblance of public scrutiny. They shun any serious discussion of critical issues: their global market dominance, price-fixing

practices in small countries, wage cuts and job losses in the third world, huge commercial debt repayments and other "negative" matters. A peak of absurdity was reached in the final preparations for the Earth Summit when there was heavy lobbying to remove the term "transnational corporations" from the draft text of Agenda 21.[9]

In 1993, shortly after this failed attempt, church coalitions[10] in the UK, Canada and the US began working on their own version of a tool of corporate responsibility. *Principles for Global Corporate Responsibility: Bench Marks for Measuring Business Performance*[11] was developed with three inter-related components. The first is a set of principles that act as a statement of business philosophy fundamental to a responsible company's actions. Second, a number of criteria flowing from the principles represent particular company policies and practices that can be compared for consistency with the principles. Finally, there is a set of "bench marks", which are specific reference points of measurement to be used in assessing the company's performance in relation to the criteria.

This framework of principles, criteria and bench marks is applied initially to the wider community, focusing specifically on ecosystems, national communities, local communities and indigenous communities. In terms of the corporate business community, the areas covered include working conditions, employed persons (women in the work-force, minority groups, persons with disabilities, child labour and forced labour), suppliers, financial integrity, ethical integrity, shareholders, joint ventures/partnerships/subsidiaries, customers and consumers.

For example, the principle, criteria and bench mark found in the section on ecosystems is as follows:

- *principle* – to minimize environmental degradation and health impacts, the "precautionary principle" is the overriding principle guiding action, shifting the burden of proof from one of proving environmental harm to one of proving environmental safety;

- *criteria* – a company-wide environmental code has been adopted and implemented;
- *bench mark* – environmental assessments are made periodically and include but are not limited to environmental impact, physical infrastructure impacts, social infrastructure impacts, cumulative (synergistic) impacts.

The three church coalitions released the first draft of these principles in 1995 and circulated it for feedback. The draft was revised on the basis of comments received from human rights, environmental and labour groups, religious institutions and companies. A second version was released in 1998 and formed the basis for a consultation with religious, social justice and environmental groups from countries of the economic South regarding its potential use as an advocacy tool in relation to the policies and practices of TNCs in their regions. The church coalitions are not asking companies to endorse the document. *Bench Marks* is meant to be used as an accountability tool through which concerned actors may evaluate companies, their codes of conduct and their implementation.

The Bench Marks project can be seen not only as a modest effort to have an impact on powerful transnational corporations through holding them more accountable but also as an ambitious initiative to try and structure humility as a spiritual value into the economic life of today's world.

NOTES

[1] David G. Hallman, *A Place in Creation: Ecological Visions in Science, Religion and Economics*, Toronto, United Church of Canada Publishing House, 1992.
[2] Lynn White, Jr, "The Historical Roots of Our Ecological Crisis", in *Science*, 155, 1967, pp.1203-207.
[3] Douglas John Hall, *The Steward: A Biblical Image Come of Age*, New York, Friendship Press, 1982.
[4] Rosemary Radford Ruether, *To Change the World: Christology and Cultural Criticism*, New York, Crossroad Books, 1981, p.67.
[5] Stan MacKay, "An Aboriginal Perspective on the Integrity of Creation", in David G. Hallman, ed., *Ecotheology: Voices from South and North*, Geneva, WCC, and Maryknoll, NY, Orbis Books, 1994.

60

6 Al-Hafiz B.A. Masri, "Islam and Ecology", in *Islam and Ecology*, London, Cassell, 1992, p.18.

7 Jean Vanier, *Becoming Human*, New York, Paulist Press, 1998.

8 Kenneth Bagnell, "Living Spiritually in a Secular Age", Toronto, *The Globe & Mail*, Saturday 9 January 1999.

9 *The New Internationalist*, no. 246, Aug. 1993, p.15.

10 The church coalitions were the Ecumenical Council for Corporate Responsibility (ECCR), a body in association with the Council of Churches for Britain and Ireland, the Taskforce on the Churches and Corporate Responsibility (TCCR) of the Canadian churches, and the Interfaith Center on Corporate Responsibility (ICCR) of the churches and faith communities of the United States.

11 Copies of the *Principles for Global Corporate Responsibility* are available through: ECCR, P.O. Box 4317, Bishop's Stortford, CM22 7GZ, UK; TCCR, 129 St Clair Ave. W., Toronto, ON, Canada M4V 1N5; ICCR, 475 Riverside Drive, Room 550, New York, NY, USA.

3. Sufficiency

And he said to them, "Take care! Be on your guard against all kinds of greed; for one's life does not consist in the abundance of possessions." "What does it profit someone to gain the whole world and lose his soul?" (Luke 12:15; 9:25).

A basic wisdom shared by many faiths is that physical well-being and spiritual fulfilment are most readily attainable through a path of moderation and the avoidance of extremes in consumption. Buddhists refer to it as the "middle way", a balance in life that seeks neither self-indulgence nor self-denial. Alan Durning in *How Much Is Enough?* quotes from the teachings of world religions and major cultures on consumption:[1]

Religion or Culture	Teaching and Source
American Indian:	"Miserable as we seem in thy eyes, we consider ourselves... much happier than thou, in this that we are very content with the little that we have" (Mi'g'ma Chief).
Buddhist:	"Whoever in this world overcomes selfish cravings, his sorrow falls away from him, like

	drops of water from a lotus flower" (Dhamma-pada, 336).
Christian:	It is "easier for a camel to go through the eye of a needle than for a rich man to enter the kingdom of God" (Matt. 19:23-24).
Confucian	"Excess and deficiency are equally at fault" (Confucius, XI.15).
Ancient Greek	"Nothing in excess" (inscribed at Oracle of Delphi).
Hindu	"That person who lives completely free from desires, without longing…attains peace" (Bhagavad-Gita, II.71).
Islamic	"Poverty is my pride" (Muhammad).
Jewish	"Give me neither poverty nor riches" (Prov. 30:8).
Taoist	"He who knows he has enough is rich" (Tao Te Ching).

While it clearly has a very long history, the spiritual value of sufficiency is gaining renewed attention today as we struggle to reduce the gap between the rich and the poor and to address the serious environmental problems posed not just by poverty but primarily by high consumption levels.

Sufficiency in terms of consumption patterns means that one has access to enough resources to provide for a good quality of life. If we think of a continuum of consumption ranging from poverty at one end to extremely high use of resources at the other, sufficiency would fall somewhere in the middle. One of the helpful aspects of the concept is that it has direct implications for each end of the continuum. Poverty must be eliminated and people must have enough food, shelter, health and education to be able to live a satisfying and productive life. But over-consumption must also be reduced. Not only do its environmental consequences threaten the quality of life for everyone but those indulging in such affluence are not finding it spiritually satisfying. As we discussed in the section on consumerism in Chapter 2, after one has reached a certain level of comfort, happiness does not increase with higher consumption rates.

Sufficiency would be a leveller among peoples. Those who are too poor to attain health, adequate nutrition, good housing and education would get the resources they need and cause less unintended environmental destruction in their struggle for survival. Those who are too rich, and whose use of much more than their fair share of the earth's resources is causing the majority of the pollution leading to environmental problems such as climate change, would have to settle for less.

In terms of environmental consequences of consumption patterns, sufficiency is an important corollary of efficiency. There has been much discussion in the context of strategies for addressing climate change of an "efficiency revolution": substantial lowering of the amount of energy that we use per unit of production or consumption. Indeed, a growing number of technological innovations would allow societies to consume much less fossil fuel while maintaining a good standard of living. This would benefit the atmosphere by reducing the amount of carbon dioxide produced by the burning of coal, oil and gas.

There have been considerable developments around the world that provide specific examples of ways in which energy efficiency and conservation can result in dramatic reductions in the amount of energy needed per unit of production and transportation:

- Super-efficient homes in Frankfurt, Germany, use 90 percent less heat and 75 percent less electricity than normal German homes.
- Super-efficient and ultra-light "hypercars" using hybrid engines can travel between 100 and 200 miles per gallon of fuel.
- An integrated transportation system in Curitiba, Brazil, has bucked the "norm" of extensive car use. With a cheap and effective bus network, 70 percent of the inhabitants use the system, leading to 30 percent lower petrol use than in other Brazilian cities.
- Clever appliance design and minimum standards-setting in Denmark can cut electricity use by 74 percent compared to 1988 levels.[2]

The work on climate change in the World Council of Churches has concluded that, as important and necessary as is the efficiency revolution, it will not be enough to meet the ecological challenge and simultaneously address the social challenge of wide disparity between the rich and the poor. What we need in addition to the efficiency revolution is a *sufficiency* revolution. By this we mean that all people would have enough for a good quality of life but not dramatically more than they need.

Key to the idea of sufficiency is the notion of quality of life. In the past, we have often spoken of quality of life in quantifiable terms. We have used "quality of life" and "standard of living" interchangeably. In fact, they are related but different. Standard of living uses basically economic measurements such as the gross national product per capita, i.e., the total output of the economy divided by the number of people among whom it will be distributed. A good standard of living can contribute significantly to a good quality of life but does not guarantee it. In fact, as many people have pursued greater and greater material wealth, they have found that their quality of life has begun to deteriorate in terms of the environmental pollution caused by industrialized societies, the stress resulting from the pressure to constantly increase their income, the loss of time for spending with family and friends, the breakdown in community, and so on.

Acceleration, both physically in the speed of movement of persons and goods and figuratively in the pace of life, is a major component of contemporary societies around the world and illustrates some of the weakness of putting too much faith in the efficiency revolution alone to solve our ecological problems. In today's world, people arrive faster and faster at places where they stay for ever shorter periods of time. Increases in the speed of travel allow us to pack our day with more and more activities but what of the quality of the time spent? In terms of carbon dioxide emissions from transportation, cars are more energy-efficient now than they were two decades ago but the gains from improved efficiency have been over-run by the dramatic increases in the

64

number of vehicles, the speed at which they are driven and the distances travelled.

Wolfgang Sachs of the Wuppertal Institute in Germany participated in one of the WCC consultations on climate change and presented some helpful perspectives on the need for a sufficiency revolution:

> The wisdom of teachings of diverse cultures in East and West may differ about the nature of the universe or the destiny of history, but almost all of them unanimously recommend cultivating the principle of simplicity in the conduct of life. That cannot just be chance. Summarizing the experiences of many generations, they end up by concluding that the way to an accomplished life does not involve the accumulation of riches. These teachings are in no way driven by masochism. They view simplicity as part of the art of living. They recognize the connection between the elegance of simplicity and the elegance of life.
>
> The opposite to a simple life-style is not luxurious existence but rather a distracted one. An over-abundance of things congests the day, distracts attention, dissipates energies and weakens the power to find a clear direction. Only by treating things cautiously do sufficient resources in the realms of time and attentiveness remain available for rightful development of a personal life-project.[3]

Faith systems have a real opportunity to provide a vision of sufficiency for the global community based on long traditions of advocating and living simpler life-styles. The monastic tradition provides not only specific practical examples of the simpler life-style but also theological and inspirational literature to support it. Religious orders to this day exemplify an understanding of sufficiency for the individual accompanied by the experiential richness of living in community.

Mennonites have been critical of the material life-style and have demonstrated their commitment to living simply. Moreover, Mennonites interpret community not only as the local gathering of families in geographic proximity but as relationships of support and solidarity that extend around the world. They attend to both ends of the sufficiency continuum

– restricting their own consumption levels while assisting persons in developing nations gain greater access to resources to meet basic needs and ensure a good quality of life. They have also demonstrated an appreciation for a North-South exchange of critical perspectives on consumption and sufficiency. In her book *Living More with Less*, Doris Janzen Longacre provides a list of potential "development projects" for North America based on suggestions by Southern partners as well as by European partners, where people maintain a high standard of living while using half or less the food and energy consumed per capita in North America:[4]

- building an energy-efficient public transportation network among small towns and cities;
- learning to cook simple, nutritious meals;
- using few kitchen appliances;
- living without disposables, setting up community systems for repair and recycling, reducing waste;
- planting home and community gardens;
- valuing family ties and friendship above making money;
- building simpler, less expensive facilities for churches.

Religious orders and Mennonites provide compelling demonstrations that people can and do choose simpler lifestyles on the basis of their faith, solidarity with the poor, commitment to the earth, and awareness of what will bring true satisfaction and fulfilment to their own lives. Beyond these groups, there is also a growing interest in "voluntary simplicity" in the broader society. Mark Burch is one of those who, often with a religious background, have written books and run workshops for people concerned about their own consumerism and anxious to discover ways of learning to live with less. Burch presents voluntary simplicity not as a choice of puritanical renunciation but rather as an act of affirmation which frees us from the evil of addictive acquisition that distracts us from what is best in our lives.

> Simplicity, then, is a decision to live more deeply. In living simply, we choose to shift our attention and effort towards a more holistic, balanced, integrated, proportionate and appropriate

66

pattern of living. This new pattern honours both the inner, non-material, aesthetic and spiritual aspects of our lives as well as their material and physical aspects. We attend to what we wear, where we live, and how we move about in the world, but also to what we say, the directness of our gaze, the singleness of our purposes in choosing our involvements and making our commitments.[5]

Incorporating the spiritual value of sufficiency into daily lives is a challenge for people in industrialized societies who have become used to all the material comforts they have accrued. There are some helpful resources that give very practical ideas about the transition towards a simpler life-style. Mark Burch has prepared a resource for group study entitled *Simplicity Study Circles: A Step-by-Step Guide.*[6] One of the critical dynamics in efforts towards just and sustainable living is that it is difficult to do so alone. Having the support of others within the family, neighbourhood, church or school makes a great difference. People can support each other emotionally and spiritually, brainstorm solutions to seemingly intractable obstacles, bring greater commitment to the decision-making, and help monitor each other's implementation of the decisions.

Another useful resource is Michael Shut's *Simplicity as Compassion: Voluntary Simplicity from a Christian Perspective.*[7] This Earth Ministry publication includes reprints of articles from various sources on worldviews, consumption patterns and eco-theology as well as programme outlines for group study on voluntary simplicity. Two interesting sessions address "food and simplicity", and "time, silence and contemplation".

One can look at the concept of sufficiency not only in terms of individual life-styles but also at the level of macro economics. In their book *For the Common Good*, Herman Daly and John Cobb Jr describe a distinction made by Aristotle between "chrematistics" and "oikonomia":

Chrematistics can be defined as that branch of political economy relating to the manipulation of property and wealth so as to maximize short-term monetary exchange value to the owner.

> Oikonomia, by contrast, is the management of the household so as to increase its use value to all members of the household over the long run.[8]

Daly and Cobb go on to note that for chrematistics, more is always better. For oikonomia, there is such a thing as enough. This is heresy in current economic ideology. The paradigm of ever-increasing economic growth fostered by global trade is accepted unquestioningly by most politicians and the general public, who have been convinced by trans-national corporations and other powerful economic actors that their jobs and standard of living are dependent on the success of this economic model.

Thinkers around the margins of the discipline of economics are proposing alternate models. In one of my earlier books, *A Place in Creation*, I reviewed some of these creative efforts, including the use of ecological systems as an example on which to base the construction of economic models for human societies. Some of the relevant characteristics as identified by Eduard Pestel in a 1989 report for the Club of Rome include:

- systematic interdependent development where no part (sub-system) grows to the detriment of the others; gains and progress in one part are real only if supported by progress in other parts;
- harmonious coordination of development goals to ensure systemwide – worldwide – compatibility;
- resilience: the ability of constituent parts to absorb disturbing influences on the course of development.[9]

Sufficiency as a spiritual value has the potential to have a pervasive impact in our individual, community and societal life-styles because of the pragmatic implications it has for our own lives and our economic systems.

A case study: sustainable mobility

How we move around in our own communities and globally presents a massive social and ecological challenge. There are vast discrepancies in the types and adequacy of transportation available to people in different regions. This is one aspect of life where the gap between the rich and the poor is most glaring. Furthermore, the style and frequency of mobility used by the wealthier members of the human community (e.g., the individually driven automobile and the airplane) are among the primary sources of pollution leading to the deterioration of air quality in urban centres and global atmospheric warming with its predicted climatic consequences. Even in poorer countries, the massive increase in urban traffic with inefficient, polluting buses and cars is endangering the health of millions.

As part of its climate change programme, the WCC has initiated a project on "sustainable mobility" in conjunction with the Evangelical Academy of Bad Boll, Germany. The resulting study paper, *Mobility: Prospects of Sustainable Mobility*,[10] provides helpful analyses and proposals for what it could mean in the transportation sector if sufficiency were to become a key organizing value. Material in this section is largely drawn from that paper.

Current transportation patterns, particularly motorized mobility, have many negative consequences including road casualties, damage to public health and the quality of life in cities, straining natural resources, placing a heavy burden on national budgets, and contributing to social injustice.

Although motorized traffic has increased rapidly, a great share of the global population remains isolated and prevented from participating in the broader society. The elderly, children, people with disabilities, and especially lower-income groups are not taken into account in the age of motorized mobility. In many countries, women in particular must do with other modes of transportation than the individual car. Since the universalization of motorized individual traffic is not feasible, the situation is unlikely to change in the near future. The ratio between a privileged elite travelling by road or by air and those depending on traditional means of transportation has remained the same over the years. Social injustice is deepened even more because traffic planning focuses mainly on individual motorized transport. Traffic planners are devoting their attention to the cities while neglecting the needs of rural areas.

In addition to the movement of people, there has been a huge increase in the transportation of goods. In a world economy that is geared increasingly to free trade, the kilometres of freight transported by plane increased by a factor of 150 between 1950 and 1998. It is estimated that truck traffic in Europe will double by the year 2010 as more and more railways are abandoned for the purposes of transporting goods in favour of roads.

In moving towards sustainable mobility, one of the important considerations must be that future generations are entitled to life opportunities undiminished from those enjoyed by the present generation. Today's generations need to act as stewards of the natural environment and to hand it over to future generations as intact as possible. Another important consideration is that all people on earth have an equal right to live in a healthy natural environment and to make use of natural resources within the carrying capacity of global ecosystems. Thus sustainable mobility deals with issues of national, international and intergenerational equity.

If mobility is to be kept within the ecological limits of God's creation, how can we calculate those limits? In the context of the climate-change science, it has been determined that the atmosphere can handle the emission of about 2000 kilogrammes of carbon dioxide per person per year. This corresponds to about 800 litres of gasoline, 700 litres of heating oil, or 3000 kwh of electricity. The industrialized nations are exceeding this per capita limit up to about ten times!

Mobility must serve the creation of sustainable communities as a whole or at least should not interfere with it. Community needs should have priority over the interests of individuals or privileged groups. Sustainable mobility is not only a matter of planning and efficiency. It presupposes a lifestyle based on values other than independence of space and time and the expectation of material gain. Sufficiency should be the operative value.

Although a shift towards sustainable mobility depends to a degree on individual behaviour change, the major focus needs to be at the systemic level so that people have sustainable options available to them. The circumstances for traffic planning differ from country to country. Every nation is confronted with the question of how an optimum degree of mobility can be achieved for everyone in the framework of national circumstances and requirements on the one hand, and the overall interests of humanity and the environment on the other hand.

The WCC/Bad Boll project identified a number of factors which could contribute to sustainable mobility:

Traffic planning:
- traffic planning must not place sole emphasis on the promotion of motorized traffic;
- the rights of pedestrians and of non-motorized transportation modes, such as bicycles, rickshaws, pack animals, and public transport should not be an afterthought but should be assigned the highest priority;
- special attention needs to be given to the requirements of rural areas.

Avoidance of mobility and shift to other modes of transport:
- the assumption needs to be challenged that goods from all over the world should be available in every part of the planet at any time;
- priority should be focused more on providing people with the goods they need from within their local area;
- rail should be given preference over other modes for the transportation of freight;
- short and mid-distance travel – under 1000 kilometres – should be accomplished through rail rather than by plane.

Technology efficiency:
- the technology already exists to produce vehicles with less raw material and energy, and much more innovation would be possible if more research resources were devoted to it;

- electric cars, hybrid fuel vehicles, and fuel-cell-driven motors should be advanced to market readiness as quickly as possible.

True costs:
- efforts should be made to calculate the true costs of various forms of transportation, including the so-called "externalities" of environmental damage and health problems; many of these costs are born by the general public;
- true cost calculations would allow mobility planning to be based on more comprehensive data.

Price increases, taxes and other fiscal measures:
- in order to internalize true costs, fuel prices must be increased considerably; this could help achieve a shift towards more sustainable mobility including rendering transportation of goods by rail more economically attractive;
- carbon taxes are being discussed in various countries as a means to reduce carbon dioxide emissions; the tax would be graduated according to the amount of carbon in the fuel source, i.e., high for coal, moderate for oil, lower for natural gas;
- if price increases and taxes are carried out through a framework of ecological tax reform, taxation on salaries could be reduced and this could lead to the creation of new jobs.

The automobile industry:
- dialogue needs to be initiated with the automobile industry because of the powerful role it plays in the promotion of the individualized car and in the economy as a whole;
- companies should be encouraged to shift towards higher efficiency and public transportation vehicles.

Emphasizing the region as expanded living space:
- the production of as many vital goods as possible should occur as close as possible to where they are needed.

72

Urban and regional design:
- as early in the planning stages as possible, urban design and infrastructure should account for the avoidance of motorized mobility;
- the requirements of pedestrians and cyclists and of women and children must rank above the interests of the automobile.

The WCC/Bad Boll study on sustainable mobility concludes with a call to the churches to become engaged with mobility issues within their local communities and with regional and national political structures as a concrete way of grounding sufficiency as a spiritual value within our lifestyles and societies.

NOTES

[1] Alan Durning, *How Much Is Enough? The Consumer Society and the Future of the Earth*, New York, W.W. Norton, 1992, p.144.
[2] See Amory Lovins, Hunter Lovins and Ernst von Weizsäcker, *Factor Four: Doubling Wealth – Halving Resource Use*, London, Earthscan, 1996.
[3] Wolfgang Sachs, "From Efficiency to Sufficiency", in *Resurgence Magazine*, no. 171, pp.6-8.
[4] Doris Janzen Longacre, *Living More with Less*, Kitchener, Canada, Herald Press, 1987, p.31.
[5] Mark A. Burch, *Simplicity: Notes, Stories and Exercises for Developing Unimaginable Wealth*, Gabriola Island, BC, Canada, New Society Publishers, 1995, pp.48-49.
[6] Mark Burch, *Simplicity Study Circles: A Step-by-Step Guide*, Gabriola Island, BC, Canada, New Society Publishers.
[7] Michael Shut, *Simplicity as Compassion: Voluntary Simplicity from a Christian Perspective*, Seattle, WA, USA, Earth Ministry, 1996.
[8] Herman Daly and John Cobb Jr, *For the Common Good: Redirecting the Economy towards Community, the Environment and a Sustainable Future*, Boston, Beacon Press, 1989, p.138.
[9] David G. Hallman, *A Place in Creation: Ecological Visions in Science, Religion and Economics*, Toronto, United Church Publishing House, 1992, p.135.
[10] WCC, *Mobility: Prospects of Sustainable Mobility*, Geneva, WCC, 1998.

4. Justice

> Is this not the fast that I choose: to loose the bonds of injustice,
> to undo the thongs of the yoke, to let the oppressed go free and
> to break every yoke? (Isa. 58:6)

The creation of sustainable communities will not happen
without a commitment to justice as a fundamental spiritual
value on the basis of which we organize our lives and our
societies. Very powerful interests actively guard the current
system that benefits the rich and penalizes the poor and the
natural world. There is a major struggle ahead to incarnate
justice as another of the fundamental spiritual values necessary for living sustainably in the 21st century.

The Judaeo-Christian scriptures and tradition understand
justice as emanating initially from God. God created this
world, loves it, and becomes engaged in it through Jesus and
the Spirit. God has entered into a covenantal relationship
with all creation so that all might enjoy life in abundance. In
return, God expects us to loose the bonds of injustice and to
work for justice. God judges with severity individuals, principalities and powers that oppress people and other elements
of God's creation.

An illustration of how God's justice relates to creation
can be found in a book already mentioned: Douglas John
Hall's *The Steward: A Biblical Symbol Come of Age.*[1] In the
Old Testament, stories of stewards revolve around their
responsibility for the well-being of the household and all its
inhabitants in the master's absence (e.g., Isa. 22). In the New
Testament, Jesus uses the steward in a metaphorical sense
(e.g., Luke 12:41-48). As noted earlier, Hall draws several
lessons from these scriptures. First, the steward does not own
the household – "The earth is the Lord's and the fullness
thereof; the world and all that dwell therein" (Ps. 24:1). Second, the steward is to look after the household as would the
master, who loves all in the household. Third, the steward
will be held responsible for how he has looked after the
household. God's judgment will be severe on the steward
who abuses the members of the household.

One of the helpful aspects of this application of the steward symbol to our relationship to creation is that it integrates all members of the household as belonging to and being loved by God, the master. Care for the well-being of people and care for the well-being of the natural world are both expectations of the covenantal relationship between God and us. Violence and oppression perpetrated against either people or nature will be judged severely by God. God's justice demands the abundant life for all and holds accountable those who deny it.

The work of theologians and ethicists from Southern countries, eco-feminist theologians and Indigenous Peoples has advanced our understanding of how God's justice interconnects the liberation of oppressed people and the liberation of the oppressed natural world.

Leonardo Boff, a Catholic liberation theologian from Brazil, critiques not only the shallow environmentalism sometimes in evidence in the North which ignores the plight of the poor but also the social justice agenda of the South which has traditionally neglected consideration of the need for a healthy ecology.[2] Boff argues for a new socio-environmental ethic to challenge those systems that exploit the poor majority in order to maintain privilege for the wealthy minority, and simultaneously to confront those systems that exploit the natural world for short-term gain. Indeed, as pointed out by Boff and others (e.g., Aruna Gnanadason, K.C. Abraham, Edward Antonio),[3] the organizations and systems that oppress the poor are often the same as those which exploit nature.

Eco-feminist theologians link the oppression of women and the oppression of nature in their analyses of justice. Elizabeth Dodson Gray[4] has identified parallels between male domination of women and the exploitation of the natural world. Gray proposes new approaches to social organization based on mutuality and interdependence. In much of her writing, Rosemary Radford Ruether takes a long historical and cultural look at the ways in which different societies have constructed myths, social systems, laws and daily practices which elevate certain privileged members and devalue others including women, children and nature. Ruether's proposals for change stress the importance of reorienting our values and redefining our theology:

> In order to create an ecological culture and society, we must transform relationships of domination and exploitation into relationships of mutual support. This transformation will not occur without a parallel change in our image of God, our image of the relationship between God and creation in all its dimensions. We must reformulate our concept of God, no longer to be seen as an imposing power that commands relationships of domination, but as a power of mutual support, the source of a true life of mutuality… Only when we have come to understand that God is the source and foundation calling us to live in relationships of mutual support can we effectively rebuild our vision of the world.[5]

Indigenous Peoples have accused the former colonial powers of Europe as well as the new-world countries in the Americas, Australia and Aotearoa New Zealand of attempted genocide of their peoples and cultures. Western societies imported into the new world a system of values, including religious mores, which viewed the Indigenous Peoples as "savages" in need of salvation or extermination. Another component of the West's model of development was an attitude towards non-human creation as simply natural resources whose only value lay in their exploitation to fuel the engines of human progress. Indigenous Peoples have contrasted this utilitarian approach to the natural world with their own long history of respect for creation. Stan MacKay, a Cree from Canada who has served both as the moderator of the United Church of Canada and in various leadership positions in the World Council of Churches, has written of the familial relationships which Indigenous Peoples have with elements in the natural world.[6] An image which MacKay and other Indigenous Peoples propose as a justice response to the exploitation of their peoples and of the earth is that of "the circle of life" in which all recognize their interdependence and live so as to help build sustainable communities.

76

There is a long history of debate within and between faith systems regarding the appropriate approach to engagement in worldly conflicts about justice. In the Christian community, some of the most assertive examples of challenging injustice in recent decades have been the efforts of churches in South Africa against the apartheid system and the liberation theologies emanating from Latin America. In both cases, "God's preferential option for the poor" has been interpreted as requiring active engagement in opposing economic, political and military oppression. We can take heart that at least some of these engagements seem to have had considerable success in changing the direction of their societies against quite overwhelming odds.

In terms of strategy, most engagements emerging from Christian theological and ethical perspectives have been nonviolent and based on the profound implications of Jesus' teachings about power. Time and time again, Jesus and the New Testament writings turn upside-down the assumed logic about power:

- Blessed are the meek, for they will inherit the kingdom of heaven (Matt. 5:3).
- At that time, the disciples came to Jesus and asked "Who is the greatest in the kingdom of heaven?" He called a child, whom he put among them, and said, "Truly I tell you, unless you change and become like children, you will never enter the kingdom of heaven" (Matt. 18:1-3).
- Whoever wants to be first, must be last of all and servant of all (Mark 9:35).
- ... for whenever I am weak, then am I strong (2 Cor. 12:10b).

The economic, political and military institutions which oppress and exploit the poor and the natural world maintain their authority through the exercise of various forms of power. Conventional logic would suggest that only greater power will be sufficient to overcome them. But the witness of these scriptures testifies to the fact that it would be a grave mistake to use similar methods of physical and economic violence to achieve justice in the world. Rather, we are called to recognize our dependence on God, seek in humility to follow the example provided by the life and teachings of Jesus, and model a new vision of living in community with all life. This is not a timid response to the powerful interests maintaining the current status quo of injustice. Quite the contrary, it requires immense courage, discernment and perseverance.

There are many examples that we can see of the power of the Holy Spirit working for justice through fragile ecumenical networks, small environmental groups, women's organizations, children and youth. These efforts are invariably organized with extremely limited financial resources. Let me cite a few examples.

- Ecumenical groups in Canada, the United Kingdom and the United States have drafted *Principles for Global Corporate Responsibility* discussed in the section on "Humility" above.[7]

- The Chipko movement, in the Utharkhand region of the Himalayas in India, is a largely tribal women-centred struggle, in which local people clung to trees in order to protect them from forestry companies.[8]

- The organizing of the climate change petition campaign by the WCC through which ecumenical networks in 23 industrialized countries built public support to pressure their governments to adopt an agreement on limiting greenhouse gas emissions at the Kyoto Climate Change Conference in December 1997.

There is a major new economic movement that threatens to create even greater injustice in the 21st century and that will severely tax our creativity and perseverance if we are to challenge it effectively. I am referring to the increasing influence of the new World Trade Organization and other bodies which are pressing for greater globalization through free trade. The agreements being negotiated through the WTO will place considerable restriction on the freedom of national governments to adopt legislation aimed at addressing environmental, social and labour problems. Such standards could be deemed as "barriers to trade" under the WTO agreements.

Indeed, countries may have to eliminate some current legislation in these areas.

The rich industrialized countries that make up the Organization for Economic Cooperation and Development (OECD) spent several years preparing a Multilateral Agreement on Investment (MAI), designed to establish a new set of global rules for investment that would grant transnational corporations the unrestricted "right" and "freedom" to buy, sell and move their operations whenever and wherever they want around the world, unfettered by government intervention or regulation. While corporations were to be granted new rights and powers under the MAI, there were no measures to ensure that corporations would maintain corresponding obligations and responsibilities regarding jobs, workers, consumers or the environment.[9] Fortunately, an international coalition of non-governmental organizations succeeded in forcing the OECD governments to become more public about the MAI negotiations. In 1998 the negotiations were abandoned, at least in part as a result of public opposition, although efforts to revive the MAI negotiations are expected within the context of the WTO. Resistance to the WTO agenda is growing among civil society groups as demonstrated by the challenges they posed both in dialogue sessions with the WTO and on the streets during the WTO meeting in Seattle in December 1999.

We are not guaranteed success in our efforts to challenge the sources of injustice and oppression in the world. Though we need to do our best to develop effective strategies, our criteria for evaluating our actions is ultimately not the success of our efforts but rather our preparedness to respond faithfully to what we understand to be the call of justice.

A case study: Climate Fund

Climate change is viewed by the WCC primarily as a justice issue between the North and the South and between the present and future generations. Churches and other organizations in the Netherlands have developed a proposal that would attempt to help reduce the potential of climate change while simultaneously recognizing the ecological debt owed by the North to the South and compensating people in the developing world for that debt.

Polluting emissions from the burning of fossil fuels are gradually warming the global atmosphere, leading to significant climatic disruptions. Over 80 percent of the human-produced carbon dioxide emissions that have accumulated in the atmosphere over the past 150 years have come from the Northern nations as they have grown wealthy through their processes of industrialization. The consequences of climate change will be suffered disproportionately by the poorer countries of the economic South and by future generations.

For many Southern countries, their geography leaves them particularly vulnerable to changes in rainfall patterns such as increasing drought in sub-Saharan Africa and rising water levels. Nations such as Bangladesh and Egypt have large populations and considerable farmland in delta areas that would become permanently flooded. Island states in the Pacific would be inundated by higher sea levels and more frequent and violent tropical storms. In addition to this geographic vulnerability, countries of the South do not have the financial resources to prepare their infrastructure for climate change. This leaves them doubly exposed to the threats posed by this problem created largely by the richer countries of the North.

Under the auspices of the United Nations, governments have been negotiating treaties to address climate change since 1989. The first major agreement was the UN Framework Convention on Climate Change (UNFCCC) adopted at the Rio Earth Summit in 1992. Two aspects of the treaty are important from a justice perspective. The governments of the world acknowledged that climate change is a global problem and thus all must work together to solve it but that some countries bear more responsibility for having precipitated it than do others. The phrase within the UNFCCC which captures this distinction is "common but differentiated responsibilities".

There is a second aspect of the treaty that is important to note here. The ultimate objective of the convention is to "achieve… stabilization of greenhouse gas concentrations in the atmosphere at a level that would prevent dangerous anthropogenic interference with the climate system".[10] To reach such a stabilization, scientists estimate that global emissions of such gases as carbon dioxide, the major greenhouse gas, will have to be reduced on an annual basis by over 60 percent. Poorer nations will likely need to continue to increase their emissions of greenhouse gases as their processes of development attempt to reduce the poverty and increase the standard of living for people in their societies. That means that the already wealthy industrialized countries will have to make dramatic reductions if the total amount of global emissions is to be lowered by over 60 percent.

The UNFCCC is a fairly general treaty without specific targets and timetables for reducing emissions. From 1995 to 1997, governments were involved in intense negotiations to come up with a more specific sub-treaty or protocol under the umbrella of the Climate Change Convention. Negotiations concluded at a major UN conference in Kyoto, Japan, in December 1997 and hence the agreement is referred to as the Kyoto Protocol.[11] The WCC delegation had the opportunity to make a statement to the Kyoto conference and framed their comments in terms of climate change as a justice issue (attached to this section).[12]

In this treaty, industrialized countries agreed to reduce their greenhouse gas emissions by an average of 5 percent from 1990 levels by the years 2010-2012. That is a far cry from over 60 percent, but at least it was a formal start to legally binding targets. Even this reduction target is not fixed, though, since the Kyoto Protocol still has to be ratified by the parliaments of the governments that signed it. The major uncertainty at the time of this writing is whether the United States Senate will agree to ratify it.

Within the Kyoto Protocol are not only the targets and timetables for emission reductions by industrialized nations but also a variety of what are euphemistically called "flexibility mechanisms". These are measures by which industrialized nations could meet part of their reduction targets not through actions to reduce fossil fuel use within their own country but through arrangements with other countries. The industrialized countries could get "credits" to be applied towards their targets by funding projects that lower emissions in another country, or by purchasing emission credits from countries that are below the target allowable for them in the Kyoto Protocol.

This may sound commendable, but the WCC and many environmental groups and Southern countries have some serious ethical reservations about the schemes. Because it may be relatively cheap to get emission reductions by funding projects in other countries where energy is used quite inefficiently, industry and governments in the richer Northern countries might feel less pressure to make reductions at home. Furthermore, the proposal for emission trading is worrisome to many in the South because it assigns an economic value to emissions, which can then be bought and sold before there is any international agreement on rights to use the atmosphere, which is one of the "global commons".[13] Southern nations are concerned that they would suffer further injustice at the hands of the North through a trading system based largely on the pattern of historical emissions in which industrialized countries have emitted far more than the developing countries. Data from 1998 illustrate the discrepancy between emissions from industrialized and from developing nations. This represents an extreme overuse by the richer nations of their fair share of the atmosphere.[14]

Country	CO_2 emissions per ton (1000 kgs) per person per year
United States	19.53
Germany	12.13
Japan	8.79
Spain	5.64
China	2.20
Brazil	1.43
India	0.81
Kenya	0.18

This is where the Dutch proposal comes in. The Climate Fund was developed by Oikos, an ecumenical development agency in the Netherlands, together with Ecooperation, a government-funded organization to promote sustainability links between the Netherlands and Southern countries.[15] The ethical premise of the Climate Fund is that the atmosphere belongs to everyone and hence each world citizen should be granted an equitable right to use it. Though there are significant differences between countries in terms of their need for energy based on climate and geography, the current discrepancies are not justifiable given the wide disparity in standard of living between the rich and the poor. The Dutch have chosen in this proposal to define "equitable right to the atmosphere" as per capita allotment in line with the proposals developed by various NGOs, especially the Centre for Science and Environment in India. For Oikos, equal per capita entitlement is not a goal in itself but a means to propel countries towards low-carbon energy strategies which will lower the emissions to the atmosphere.

The ultimate aim of the Climate Fund is to cut CO_2 emissions in half and distribute them equally. For the world as a whole, average per capita emissions are currently about 4 tons per year. Scientists estimate that the atmosphere can absorb about 2 tons per person per year and recycle it without serious disruption of the climate system. The Climate Fund is an innovative approach to encourage individuals, industry, organizations and governments in industrialized countries to take action to reduce their emissions and for the poorer nations to keep their emissions low by pursuing development strategies that rely on less polluting energy sources.

Participants in the Climate Fund would commit themselves to paying compensation for emissions that exceed 2 tons per person. The cost of the excess emissions would be pegged at about US$15 a ton, which is an average figure drawn from various economic studies of damage caused per ton of CO_2 and the costs of emissions reduction. For instance, the average per capita emissions in the Netherlands currently total about 11.3 tons. The Netherlands would thus need to make drastic efforts to reduce emissions to two tons per capita while in the meantime paying compensation to the world community for the difference between entitlements and actual emissions. At a price of US$15 per ton, the Dutch annual compensation would amount to US$139.50 per person. People would receive simple tools that would allow them to calculate their CO_2 emissions based on their living situation, consumption patterns, travel, and so on.

Oikos and Ecooperation are launching the Climate Fund initially on a voluntary approach, hoping that people, businesses, organizations such as churches, and governments would be convinced by the ethical argument that it is the right thing to do. A lot of time, education and discussion will obviously be needed to encourage people to participate, but positive feedback has come from various sectors.

The organizers are still working on how the funds raised would be distributed to those countries whose per capita emissions are well below the allowable 2 tons per person per year. The intention is that the capital transferred would facilitate patterns of development in countries of the South that avoid the fossil fuel-intensive and polluting path of industrialization that characterized the history of Northern countries. Thus both Northern and Southern nations would have economic incentives to pursue sustainable development paths.

Though there may be many obstacles encountered by the organizers in trying to launch the Climate Fund, it does represent a creative approach to building justice into our ecological and social relationships as a global community.

Statement of the WCC Delegation to the
High Level Segment of the Third Session
of the Conference of the Parties (COP3)
to the UN Framework Convention on Climate Change
Kyoto, Japan, 9 December 1997

...We make this statement on behalf of the World Council of Churches with a combination of humility and prayer, wanting to assist the process and yet needing to speak the truth as we discern it.

For us in the World Council of Churches, the core of the COP3 agenda is *justice*.

Justice means being held responsible for one's actions. The rich of the world, through promotion of the current economic model, have been and continue to be responsible for the vast majority of emissions causing human-produced climate change but seem unwilling to honestly acknowledge that responsibility and translate it into action. It is ironic that countries which exult in their domestic legal principles feel themselves above the law when it comes to their international obligations on climate change.

Justice means being held accountable for promises you make. The rich of the world have broken their Rio promise to stabilize emissions by 2000 at 1990 levels and yet seem to exhibit no embarrassment at their failure.

Justice means being held responsible for the suffering you cause to others. Small island states, millions of environmental refugees and future generations will suffer as a result of the callous exploitation of the earth's resources by the rich.

Justice means being held accountable for abuse of power. Human societies, particularly in the over-developed countries, are damaging the environment through climate change with little respect for the inherent worth of other species which we believe to be loved by God as are we.

Justice means an equitable sharing of the earth's resources. Millions of people lack the necessities for a decent quality of life. It is the height of arrogance to propose that restrictive commitments be placed on the poor to make up for the delinquencies of the rich. Over-consumption of the rich and poverty of the poor must both be eliminated to ensure quality of life for all.

Justice demands truth. Destructive misinformation campaigns are being used by groups with powerful economic self-interest with the intention of preventing meaningful action on climate change.

Justice requires honesty. The world is not so easily divided into the rich North and the poor South as we used to think. There are a few wealthy and powerful countries and elites within the category referred to as developing countries who sometimes misuse this classification of nations to disguise their economic self-interest.

God's justice is strict but it is not cruel. We are all here in Kyoto as brothers and sisters equal before God within the community of creation – a creation which we all want to be healthy and thriving for future generations. In affirmation of the goodness of creation (Gen.1:25), God beckons us to respect all forms of life. In what we do at COP3, we must not betray life.

Confidence-building measures are needed so that together we can reduce the threat of climate change:

- Industrialized countries must demonstrate, in the near future, real and significant reductions in domestic greenhouse gas emissions which many studies have shown to be possible with a considerable net benefit to their economies.
- Though developing countries should not be subject to formal emission limitation commitments yet, many of them are pursuing measures and can continue their efforts to become more energy-efficient and to limit greenhouse gas emissions.
- The sharing of finance and technological resources is needed but it is also very important to exchange experiences from both South and North including those of indigenous cultures, women's organizations and others which can offer lessons and tools for learning to live in a socially just, equitable and ecologically sustainable manner.

In these remaining days of COP3, let us shift our energies away from trying to figure out how to attain the minimum and channel them instead towards creative risk-taking options for accomplishing the maximum. Thank you.

NOTES

1 Douglas John Hall, *The Steward: A Biblical Symbol Come of Age*, New York, Friendship Press, 1982.
2 Leonardo Boff, "Social Ecology: Poverty and Misery", in David G. Hallman, ed., *Ecotheology: Voices from South and North*, Geneva, WCC Publications, and Marynoll, NY, Orbis Books, 1994. Also see Leonardo Boff, *Cry of the Poor, Cry of the Land*, Marynoll, NY, Orbis Books, 1997.
3 Aruna Gnanadason, "Women, Economy and Ecology", K.C. Abraham, "A Theological response to the Ecological Crisis", and Edward Antonio, "Letting People Decide: Toward an Ethic of Ecological Survival in Africa", in Hallman, *Ecotheology*.
4 Elizabeth Dodson Gray, *Green Paradise Lost*, Wellesley, MA, Roundtable Press, 1981.
5 Rosemary Radford Ruether, "Eco-feminism and Theology", in Hallman, *Ecotheology,* p.204.

[6] Stan MacKay, "An Aboriginal Perspective on the Integrity of Creation", in Hallman, *Ecotheology*.

[7] *Benchmarks: Principles for Global Corporate Responsibility* is available from the Taskforce on the Churches and Corporate Responsibility, 129 St Clair Ave. W., Toronto, Canada M4V 1N5.

[8] The Chipko movement has been described by various writers including in the article by Gnanadason "Women, Economy and Ecology", in Hallman, *Ecotheology*.

[9] More information on the Multilateral Agreement on Investment can be provided through many non-governmental organizations working on trade issues as well as in a document of the Canadian churches entitled "Toward Sustainable Community – Five Years since the Rio Earth Summit", 1997 (available from the author).

[10] *United Nations Framework Convention on Climate Change*, article 2, New York, UN, 1992.

[11] See Sebastian Oberthür and Hermann E. Ott, *The Kyoto Protocol: International Climate Policy for the 21st Century*, Berlin, Springer-Verlag, 1999.

[12] In addition to the WCC, many other non-governmental organizations made important statements to the Kyoto conference. They have been compiled by Azza Taalab in *Rising Voices against Global Warming*, Frankfurt, IZE, 1998.

[13] Some of the best resource material on equity issues related to the Kyoto Protocol have been developed by the Centre for Science and Environment, 41 Tughlakabad Institutional Area, New Delhi 110 062:
The Atmospheric Rights of All People on Earth
The Kyoto Protocol – What Does it Really Say?

[14] Michael Carley and Philippe Spapens, *Sharing the World: Sustainable Living and Global Equity in the 21st Century*, London, Earthscan, 1998, reproduced in "Proposal for the Establishment of a Climate Fund", Utrecht, Netherlands, Oikos, 1998.

[15] Material in this section is drawn from "Proposal for the Establishment of a Climate Fund" and *Share and Share Alike: New Ways Forward*, Oikos Memorandum, Utrecht, Oikos, 1998.

5. Love

> This is my commandment, that you love one another as I have loved you. No one has greater love than this, to lay down one's life for one's friends. You are my friends if you do what I command you (John 15:12-14).

Love is an obvious spiritual value that would be essential as part of the foundation for just and sustainable living. But being obvious does not mean that it is an easy or comfortable value on which to base our life-styles or societies. If we look at the Christian scriptures, we read of a demanding and challenging value. To love one another as Jesus has loved us is quite an intimidating commandment. Jesus died for us. He gave up his life so that we could be united with God and experience life in all its abundance. Do we have that kind of love for one another?

I want to explore two aspects of this commandment: who are the "one another", "friends", or "neighbours" that we are to love as Jesus loved us, and what does it mean to die or lay down our life for them?

Jesus taught us that "you shall love your neighbour as yourself" (Matt. 22:39), and throughout his ministry he continuously expanded the definition of neighbour. Neighbour does not mean just those near us or those with whom we get along. For Jesus, the neighbour was the woman at the well who belonged to a different people, the victim of violence assisted by the Good Samaritan, the woman caught in adultery. The neighbour is anyone in need.

In our day, there are many in need. The gap between the rich and the poor continues to grow. This is the case between countries where the wealth of the richest nations is rising and the poverty of the poorest is increasing. Per capita income in the United States has increased from $8700 in 1957 to over $20,000 today.[1] By contrast, average incomes in some of the poorer developing countries remain in the range of several hundreds of dollars annually. International debt imposes an incredible burden on many countries especially in Africa. Kenya spends about 25 percent of its government revenue on debt service payments, compared with 6.8 percent on education and 2.7 percent on health.[2]

Economic inequality is growing within many countries as well as between them. In the United States, the proportion of families earning more than $60,000 (in 1995 dollars) has increased from 20 percent in 1970 to 25 percent in 1995 while the number of families earning under $20,000 has also risen from 20 percent to 25 percent.[3]

The growing gap between rich and poor undermines efforts to create sustainable communities which require, by definition, socio-economic justice as a foundation. What can we do to express love in the context of such inequity? At the international level, millions of people have participated in the Jubilee Debt Petition Campaign, which has pressured governments in industrialized countries, banks and international financial institutions to forgive major amounts of the debt owed by the poorest of the developing nations. The lenders were taken by surprise at the size of the campaign and the number of ordinary citizens who became involved. Government leaders agreed to actions that very likely would not have occurred without the campaign. The concessions granted by the lending governments have not been as generous or just as the Jubilee Campaign wanted, and their efforts in support of these poorest nations continue in various forms. The campaign has been led by churches and non-governmental organizations and is an example of how public organizing can make a difference and can change political and social policy of governments and commercial enterprises.

At a national or local level, expressing love for our neighbour can take many tangible forms. Many local churches are actively involved in projects to assist the hungry and destitute. But these risk becoming endless "band-aid" responses if not supplemented with advocacy efforts to change the social and economic policies of governments towards greater equity. One of the politically popular movements in many industrialized countries currently is tax cuts. Conservative politicians are prepared to limit support for social programmes, health care and education in order to provide cuts in taxes, which invariably seem to provide more benefit to wealthy individuals and corporations than to the poor. Expressing love for our neighbour not only means supporting a food bank but also opposing tax policies which exacerbate the gap between rich and poor.

Working for the well-being of earth community integrates concerns for social justice and for ecological integrity. Hence, our biblical understanding of who is our neighbour is expanding beyond the human family to recognize that all life is inter-related and our health is dependent on the health of the broader ecosystem. The spirituality of Aboriginal Peoples provides insights based on traditions that go far beyond that of most peoples of European descent:

> The conspicuous absence of an all-embracing term for "non-human" creatures suggests that, in the world of the Chewong (aboriginal peoples of Malaysia), human beings are only one species among many different kinds of animate creatures. As a result, the Chewong do not divide the world into human versus the rest of nature and supernature.[4]
>
> The spritual connection between the Gitksan people (in British Columbia, Canada) and their traditional territories is captured in the totem poles... Each Gitksan pole recreates, by reaching upward, the link with the spirit forces that give the people their power... Its roots spread out into the land, thereby linking man, spirit power, and the land so they form a living whole.[5]

This traditional wisdom is being rediscovered in the modern science of ecology, which documents the interconnections between life-forms. Christian theology and life need to catch up and learn to practise love to our neighbours throughout the natural world. My own denomination, the United Church of Canada, has taken steps to reflect this understanding in our creed by adding a phrase that refers specifically to our place within the broader natural world:

> We are called to be the church:
>> to celebrate God's presence,
>> *to live with respect in creation*,
>> to love and serve others,
>> to seek justice and resist evil,
>> to proclaim Jesus, crucified and risen,
>>> our judge and our hope...[6]

We may learn from science about the interconnections of all life forms and we may appreciate from other cultures, especially Indigenous Peoples, the rich imagery of members of the natural world being part of our family. We may even adapt our theology and liturgies to express that connection.

But love is a dynamic that touches our whole being – our intellect and our emotions, our physical bodies and our souls. To love the natural world is not only to be rationally convinced of its inherent worth but to be engaged with it so that we express and receive affection emotionally, physically, spiritually. In the wonder that is creation, we can experience this power of love at the macro level viewing the galaxies of stars or a stunning sunset or we can be touched by a single bloom or a baby sparrow. Love involves our whole being, and the sooner we can develop relationships of love with nature, the sooner we can appreciate the urgency and profound implications of earth community.

If we see the natural world as our neighbour and friend, what does it mean to love it as we love ourselves and to love it as God has loved us? Love can be demonstrated by caring for the earth's well-being and seeking to avoid the unnecessary suffering of other life-forms. That is easier expressed than accomplished, especially when we encounter situations that seem to require an assault in some form upon the natural world in order to meet human needs for food, shelter and clothing. Environmental ethicists have struggled with this dilemma and have developed a process to help in complex decision-making. The first step is to assess whether the proposed action is intended to meet a genuine human need or whether it is responding to an unessential human desire. If the need really is necessary for a good quality of life, then the second step is to determine whether that human need can be met in another way than having to disrupt or destroy part of the natural world. If no options are available, then the third step is to explore ways of minimizing as much as possible the disruptive impact. Only once such steps are taken in a conscientious and responsible manner is it considered ethically justifiable to place the meeting of that human need over the well-being of that part of the natural world.

Love as a basic spiritual value gets even more challenging than just caring for our neighbour. Jesus taught that "you have heard it said, 'You shall love your neighbour and hate your enemy.' But I say to you, 'Love your enemies and pray for those who persecute you'" (Matt. 5:44). The imagery of "enemy" is problematic. Much of Jesus' ministry and teaching was directed towards forcing us to re-evaluate our assumptions and labelling of others as the enemy. Now here in this passage from Matthew's gospel, we have Jesus talking about enemies. But perhaps this is not as inconsistent at it appears on the surface because, however the others are called, Jesus' admonition to us is to love them.

In the context of our efforts towards just and sustainable community, I suppose that our "enemies" would be those who are actively engaged in policies and practices that promote materialistic consumption, exploitative economic globalization and violence. Most people are caught up in our contemporary economic systems because of the need for a job and are hence inadvertent agents of consumerism and globalization. That certainly doesn't qualify them for the designation as enemy. Probably more relevant are those people with significant economic and political power who are designing and directing the systems which promote consumerism and economic globalization and those persons who intentionally precipitate systemic violence.

What Jesus requires of us is not to demonize them as enemy but rather to respect all as children of God and to love them. Loving them does not mean we have to agree with them or acquiesce to their agenda. Indeed, our commitment to earth community requires us to challenge their ideas and actions and to work energetically to transform into sustainable communities the systems that they have created. That means engaging the corporate executive, the international trade official, the government minister of finance and confronting them with the analysis and vision of earth community. It means working in solidarity with the poor, the marginalized, exploited nature and those most victimized by the current systems so that their neglected voices are heard by the powerful and a place is opened at the table for them to participate in the creation of sustainable communities.

Is it not a naive, romanticized approach to social transformation to seek to engage the powerful along with the powerless? Are not the vested economic and political interests so firmly entrenched that any "engagement" on their part with those of us committed to just and sustainable community is likely to be some form of coopting of our energies so as to reduce opposition to their objectives?

I think that Jesus leaves us little choice. Love as a foundational spiritual value in our commitment to earth community requires an openness to the Spirit of God working in unexpected places and through the unlikeliest of people. Other faiths have perspectives to offer that can help us with such complexities. From the beginning, Buddhism has been a religion of merchants. The Buddha spoke with kings and secured large donations from merchants. A key supporter of the Buddha was the money changer Anathapindika, who provided the Buddha and his disciples with a retreat. Buddhists depended on merchants and directed much of their teaching towards them. Lewis Lancaster observes that,

> ... this indicates that we have a very different perception regarding wealth and merchants in Buddhism than we do in Western cultural systems... If ecological discourse assumes a rejection of this particular group, then one of the pillars of the Buddhist community will be under strong attack. Perhaps we can learn from Buddhism in this regard. We need to seek out the merchants and the corporate leaders, include them in our conferences, urge them to become active partners in the search for answers to the ecological crisis.[7]

The challenge for us is to maintain our vision of earth community so that we are not seduced by the forces of those who would subvert that vision.

Several things help us maintain our vision. The first is to be grounded firmly in the life experience of those most oppressed by the current economic and social systems. We need to listen to the stories, analyses and proposals for change articulated by Aboriginal Peoples, agricultural workers, visible minorities, inner-city poor, abused women and children, and others. They should have roles of leadership in analyzing the problems and developing strategies of response.

We also need increased clarity on what constitutes sustainable community to help us chart our way. There are lessons from Aboriginal Peoples and from countries of the South, especially the women, who have understood the critical factors in creating and maintaining homes and communities that allow for full participation of all and function within the carrying capacity of the ecosystems around them. Many groups within civil society both in the North and the South are developing proposals and testing models for sustainable community. Theological and ethical reflection by ecumenical organizations such as the WCC is helping to deepen the value base on which sustainable communities can be built.

Our vision of earth community can be further maintained through a recognition that we are not alone. God is with us and the broad community of creation is with us. The powerful bond bringing us together with God and with creation is love. Love can be understood as the essential element for building sustainable community within the human family and the broader creation.

So far we have been looking at who might be our friends, neighbours and even our "enemies", whom we are called to love. Now let us turn to consider what Jesus might mean for us today "to lay down one's life for one's friends". Jesus' words demolish any sense that love as a spiritual value essential for earth community is facile or frivolous – loving unto death, our own death for the sake of one's friend.

Such dying can occur in various ways. One might lay down one's life in the pursuit of political, social or economic justice for our own or for another's community. The struggles against apartheid in South Africa or military dictatorships in Latin America figure among the clearest examples from the latter part of the 20th century. Peace and human rights activists have been killed in the cause of freedom and common security. Development and emergency aid workers have given their lives trying to save others. There have also been those who have died in defence of nature, protecting the rainforests and the livelihood of Indigenous Peoples in the

Amazon. Buddhist monks have been killed protecting forests in Southeast Asia.

Not many of us will find ourselves in situations during our lives where we feel called physically to lay down our life for our friend. But I suspect that we are all called everyday to lay down those aspects of our lives which inhibit our friend from experiencing the abundant life Jesus promised. The life that we are invited to lay down is that which is addicted to consumerism, acquiesces to globalization and fosters violence. Though not as final as physical death, dying to the life that runs counter to earth community is an ongoing, indeed life-long process. But it is not a death that we will mourn – not if we are truly in touch with the gifts that we, and our friend, will experience with a world founded on spiritual values such as gratitude, sufficiency, justice and peace.

Christians are called to anticipate the just and loving community, the shalom that God wills and promises. We build sustainable community to the degree that we are able to exemplify the difficult yet joyous love about which Jesus spoke.

A case study: Community Shared Agriculture[8]

Food is an essential human need that links us to others in the human community and to the natural world. It is not some magically appearing substance but rather the product of farmers' hard labour drawing on the processes of soil, rain and sun. Community Shared Agriculture (CSA) is a means of nurturing relationships between those who produce and those who consume farm produce in ways that respect the integrity of the environment. CSA is one way to help build just and sustainable communities – to incorporate the spiritual value of love in our collective lives.

CSA (referred to as community "shared" agriculture by some and community "supported" agriculture by others) is a unique model of local agriculture whose roots reach back thirty years to Japan. A group of Japanese women, concerned about the increase in food imports and the corresponding decrease in the farming population, initiated a direct growing and purchasing relationship between their group and local farms. This arrangement, called *teikei* in Japanese, translates to "putting the farmers' face on food". The concept travelled to Europe and was adapted to the United States and given the name Community Supported Agriculture in 1985. As of January 1999, there are over 1000 CSA farms across the US and Canada.

There are a range of social, economic and environmental problems with the way in which most food production and distribution occurs in contemporary Western societies. In the US, food travels an average of 1300 miles from the farm to the market shelf. Transportation of so much food over such long distances contributes a substantial amount of polluting emissions to the atmosphere. Almost every state in the US buys 85-90 percent of its food from elsewhere. University of Massachusetts studies have determined that Massachusetts could produce about 35 percent of its food supply – a 20 percent increase that would contribute $1 billion annually to the state.

Meanwhile, the best farm land is being lost to commercial and residential development at an accelerating rate. At the same time, the retirement of older farmers, increasing land and production costs, low food prices, competing land uses, the lack of incentive for young people to enter farming, and the fundamental restructuring of the national and global economy all combine to make farming and local food production an increasingly difficult task. CSA represents a viable alternative to the prevailing situation and the long-distance relationship most of us have with the food we eat.

CSA reflects an innovative and resourceful strategy to connect local farmers with local consumers, develop a regional food supply and strong local economy, maintain a sense of community, encourage land stewardship, and honour the knowledge and experience of growers and producers working with small to medium farms. CSA is a partnership of mutual commitment between a farm and a community of supporters which provides a direct link between the production and consumption of food. Supporters cover a farm's yearly operating budget by purchasing a share of the season's harvest. CSA members make a commitment to support the farm throughout the season, and assume the costs, risks and bounty of growing food along with the farmer or grower. Members help pay for seeds, fertilizer, water, equipment maintenance and labour. In return, the farm provides, to the best of its ability, a healthy supply of seasonal fresh produce throughout the growing season. Becoming a member creates a responsible relationship between people and the food they eat, the land on which it is grown and those who grow it.

This mutually supportive relationship between local farmers, growers and community members helps create an economically stable farm operation in which members are assured the highest quality produce, often at below retail prices. In return, farmers and growers are guaranteed a reliable market for a diverse selection of crops.

Celia Guilford describes the initiation of Community Shared Agriculture in Canada:[9]

> On 5 and 6 March 1993, a crowd of 200 gathered together for Manitoba's first workshop on Community Shared Agriculture. "People and the land", they called it, "sharing the vision" for both farmers and city people. And people came from all across Canada and some from the States as well. They wanted to put the culture back in agriculture.
>
> Two main forces behind this event were Dan and Wilma Wiens from St Adolphe, Manitoba. The Wienses began operating their CSA farm in the spring of 1992. It was the first of its kind on the prairies, and within one day of local media coverage, over 200 people had signed up for a $140 share in their harvest.
>
> Two hundred families have bought shares in the Wienses' farm for two years now. These people have family doctors and lawyers; now they have a family farmer.
>
> CSA offers benefits to both farmers and the consumers. The farmers get full retail price for the food they grow; they have a guaranteed market, with income upfront, thereby reducing the need for bank loans; and they have the opportunity to get to know the people they grow food for. The consumers feel empowered because their food dollars go directly to the farm-

ers, supporting a local economy; the fresh produce they receive is grown organically; and the variety changes with the season so that it is a learning experience as well. In getting to know their farmers, consumers feel good about where their food comes from.

As one of the Wienses' sharers said at the end of last year's season, "This isn't about an economic arrangement between the farmer and the urbanite. It's about friendship."

More specifically, how does CSA work? A farmer or grower, often with the assistance of a core group, draws up a budget reflecting the production costs for the year. This includes all salaries, distribution costs, investments for seeds and tools, land payments, machinery maintenance and other expenses. The budget is then divided by the number of people for which the farm will provide. This determines the cost of each share of the harvest. One share is usually designed to provide the weekly vegetable needs for a family of four. Flowers, fruit, meat, honey, eggs and dairy products are also available through some CSAs.

Community members sign up and purchase their shares, either in one lump sum before the seeds are sown in early spring, or in several instalments throughout the growing season. Production expenses are thereby guaranteed and the farmer or grower starts receiving income as soon as work begins. In return for their investment, CSA members receive a bag of fresh, locally-grown, typically organic produce once a week from late spring through early fall, and occasionally throughout the winter in Northern climates and year-round in milder zones. Members prefer a wide variety of vegetables and herbs, which encourages integrated cropping and companion planting. These practices help reduce risk factors and give multiple benefits to the soil. Crops are planted in succession in order to provide a continuous weekly supply of mixed vegetables. As crops rotate throughout the season, weekly shares vary by size and types of produce, reflecting local growing seasons and conditions.

CSAs vary considerably according to the farm or garden location, agricultural practices, and specific farm and community goals and needs. Memberships are known to embrace a variety of community members, including low-income families, homeless people, senior citizens and differently-abled individuals. If provided, an extra fee typically is charged for home delivery. Most CSAs invite members to visit the farm and welcome volunteer assistance. Working shares are an option in some cases: a member commits three or four hours a week to help the farm in exchange for a discount on membership cost.

Apprenticeships are growing in popularity on many CSAs. For some farms they are an integral component of a successful operation. Apprenticeships offer valuable hands-on education.

Property arrangements tend to be quite flexible. Beyond private ownership, there is leasing of land with lease fees factored in as a regular budget item. CSA is also an excellent opportunity for holding land in some form of trust arrangement.

Every CSA strives over time for a truly sustainable operation, both economically and environmentally. Many try to develop to their highest potential by expanding to provide additional food items such as honey, fruit, meats and eggs. Networks of CSAs have been forming to develop associative economies by growing and providing a greater range of products in a cooperative fashion.

Some CSAs provide produce for local restaurants, roadside stands or farmers' markets while building farm membership or, in many cases, in addition to it.

Several advantages to the direct marketing approach of CSA, in addition to shared risk and pre-payment of farm costs, are the minimal loss and waste of harvested farm produce, little or reduced need for long-term storage, and a willingness by members to accept produce with natural cosmetic imperfections.

Often, a core group made up of the farmers or growers, distributors and other key administrators, and several CSA members make up the decision-making body for CSA determining short and long-range goals, preparing the budget, conducting publicity and outreach, organizing events, and so on. Annual meetings, a member newsletter, and occasional surveys are some basic means of communication between the farm and its members.

Why is community supported agriculture important?

- CSA's direct marketing gives farmers and growers the fairest return on their products.
- CSA keeps food dollars in the local community and contributes to the maintenance and establishment of regional food production.
- CSA encourages communication and cooperation among farmers. With a "guaranteed market" for their produce, farmers can invest their time in doing the best job they can rather than looking for buyers.
- CSA supports the biodiversity of a given area and the diversity of agriculture through the preservation of small farms producing a wide variety of crops.
- CSA creates opportunity for dialogue between farmers and consumers.
- CSA creates a sense of social responsibility and stewardship of local land.
- CSA puts "the farmers' face on food" and increases understanding of how, where and by whom our food is grown.

NOTES

[1] David Myers, "Money & Misery", in Rodney Clapp, ed., *Consuming Passion: Christianity & the Consumer Culture*, Downers Grove, IL, InterVarsity Press, 1998, p.58.
[2] Lester Brown, et al, *Vital Signs 1999*, New York, W.W. Norton, 1999, p.66.
[3] Myers, "Money & Misery", p.62.
[4] Peter Knudtson and David Suzuki, *Wisdom of the Elders*, Toronto, Stoddart, 1992, p.90.
[5] *Ibid.*, p.128.
[6] United Church of Canada, "A New Creed", in *Voices United*, Toronto, United Church of Canada Publishing House, 1996.

100

[7] Lewis Lancaster, "Buddhism and Ecology: Collective Cultural Perceptions", in *Buddhism and Ecology: The Interconnection of Dharma
and Deeds,* Mary Evelyn Tucker and Duncan Ryuken Williams, eds,
Harvard University Centre for the Study of World Religions, 1997,
pp.9-10.

[8] Material in this section is drawn largely from an article on Community
Supported Agriculture on a web site of the University of Massachusetts (www.umass.edu/umext/csa).

[9] Excerpts from Celia Guilford, *CSA Prairie Pioneers: Dan and Wilma
Wiens*, appearing on a web page of McGill University, Ecological
Agriculture Projects (www.eap.mcgill.ca).

6. Peace

Do not think that I have come to bring peace to the earth;
I have not come to bring peace, but a sword (Matt. 10:34).

Peace I leave with you; my peace I give to you.
I do not give to you as the world gives.
Do not let your hearts be troubled,
and do not let them be afraid (John 14:27).

Jesus seems to be saying contradictory things about
peace. Did he come to bring peace or not?

These two verses are actually quite compatible if we recognize that Jesus was speaking about peace not as an isolated
spiritual value but as one that is inextricably related to other
values such as justice and love. The peace that Jesus brings
is not a weak, compliant resignation but rather a tough,
assertive pursuit of wholeness for individuals and for communities.

The Matthew passage about peace and a sword continues
with exhortations from Jesus that "whoever loves father or
mother more than me is not worthy of me", and "whoever
does not take up the cross and follow me is not worthy of
me" (Matt. 10:37a,38). These are exacting demands. Jesus is
here reiterating what is said elsewhere throughout the scriptures: that faith in God requires an all-encompassing commitment to Jesus and his teachings – a commitment which
reaches into every aspect of our lives and which takes precedence over everything else.

If we take up the cross, it means that we will be follow-ing the example and teaching of Jesus. We will be working for earth community so that all may have life in abundance. We will be challenging those forces which oppress the poor and the marginalized among God's creatures, human and non-human. Those forces may be the principalities and pow-ers of corporate structures and global economic institutions or it may be that "one's foes will be members of one's own household" (Matt. 10:36). Taking up the cross necessitates discernment on our part to perceive what is required of us and demands strength to be willing to follow through regard-less where it leads.

It may lead to death. Jesus' discussion on peace in this section of Matthew's gospel concludes with the alarming warning that "those who will find their life will lose it, and those who lose their life for my sake will find it" (Matt. 10:39). History records the struggles unto death of martyrs. Many more who lose their lives in struggles for justice, peace and the protection of God's creation go unrecognized.

The losing of one's life for Jesus' sake may also be a non-physical death. It may be the loss of a way of life. Jesus could be calling us to give up a way of life that runs counter to the well-being of God's creation – the losing of our life for his sake and the sake of those he loves. In losing our life for his sake, we are not left with nothing but indeed with *life* itself, the abundant life that Jesus brings.

Buddhism has a deep understanding of the abundant life as spiritual fulfilment experienced through living in peaceful relationships with the entirety of creation. There are various branches of Buddhism whose traditions and teachings differ one from another, including in their implications for ecolog-ical concern. Classical Buddhism in India, its place of origin, exemplifies serious reservations about the natural world. In many texts from Indian Buddhism, reference is made to the terrible and frightening forests, to the wilderness infested with robbers, vermin, beasts of prey and flesh-eating ghouls.

This hostility towards the natural world can be under-stood in part by appreciating the context in which the Buddha lived. While the Buddha was a wandering ascetic, he nonetheless taught and lived in the growing urban world of his time. He lived his childhood in a city, and his view of the forests as places of danger and suffering was likely influenced by that. This is not to say that contact with wild nature is to be avoided. In the Perfection of Wisdom literature *(Prajna-paramita)* we find that the *bodhisattva* (exemplar of practice) believes that by experiencing the agonies of the jungle, one can develop compassion for those forced to live lives where they experience constant danger. Nevertheless, in the final analysis, the *bodhisattva* vows that in Buddha land, which will be created at the time of his elevation to Buddhahood, there will be no animals, the inhabitants will eat only divine food and there will be plenty of water. Buddha land will be like a pleasure grove near a great city.

Indian Buddhism, however, does not reflect only this reserved attitude towards nature. In the *Jataka*, or birth stories, we find that one of the reasons to follow Buddha is that for lifetime after lifetime he has expressed his compassion for animals and other beings. Christopher Key Chapple has analyzed the 550 birth stories accepted within the Theravada tradition, each of which tells about a past life of the Buddha and includes a moral lesson. Half of these stories include animals, often as central characters, including former incarnations of the Buddha. The moral lessons of the stories teach the importance of values such as generosity, gratitude and the protection of life. The birth stories involving animals interconnect with the Buddhist belief in reincarnation by illustrating how present life will continue in some future form. Further,

> because lives have endured so many incarnations, a familial link may be assumed... Repeated birth generates an interconnected web of life which, according to the Buddhist precept of harmlessness, must be respected.[1]

Contrary to the fearsome images about the natural world in Indian Buddhism, Chinese Buddhism seems to revere nature. The contrast in perspectives illumines some of the dynamics of how religions and the representation of their spiritual values evolve as a function of different cultural contexts when they move into different regions. The specific teachings may vary in relation to the social context, but spiritual values such as peacefulness remain central.

By the time that Buddhism reached China, most of the kingdom had been deforested and domesticated for agriculture. Nature was thus perceived as those isolated islands of mountains within a sea of cultivated fields. In fact, it was the practice among the sages of China to leave the cultivated areas and retreat to the mountains in search of wisdom.

The Chinese had long believed that contact with nature was important and could be a source of healing and spiritual nourishment. But they had no adequate way to explain this dynamic. In Buddhism, they were able to find an explanation for this deep connection: the concept of Buddha-nature. Every person has Buddha-nature, but what is important for one's understanding of nature is that all other sentient beings and insentient objects also have Buddha-nature – rocks, streams, trees, lotuses, mountains. Chinese Buddhist poetry and art became an attempt to capture this essence of nature, its Buddha-nature.

Buddhist teaching moves further to provide more concrete guidance for living in peaceful harmony with one's life and the universe. As described by John Daido Loori,[2] the 16 Precepts can be readily applied to our relationships with the natural world even though they have been traditionally interpreted in terms of one's relationship with other people. The Precepts include such teachings as:

- not creating evil;
- practising good;
- actualizing good for others;
- affirming life – not killing;
- manifesting truth – not lying;
- giving generously – not being withholding;
- experiencing the intimacy of things.

According to Loori, practising the Precepts means being fully conscious of what they mean and their implications for

104

one's life. It also requires an honesty with oneself in assessing the degree to which one is living out their intention. There is an empowerment which accompanies practising the Precepts, allowing one to take responsibility for one's own life and thereby to gain a sense of empowerment. "To take responsibility means to acknowledge yourself as the master of your life."[3] This effectively eliminates excuses of blaming others or denying culpability for our role in damaging the environment and should impel us to do our best to protect it.

For Christians, it is in the context of our commitment to love and serve Jesus even unto death that we can appreciate the nature of the peace which Jesus promises. It is not the peace that the world offers. That wordly peace comes in various guises these days. Materialism abetted by incessant advertising is calculated to dull us into becoming mindless consumers. Our needs can be met by this gadget. Our pain can be relieved with that product. Our longings and desires can be assuaged by this purchase. Peace is portrayed as satiation.

At another level, worldly peace is trumpeted these days as prosperity through economic growth. Subscribe unquestioningly to an ideology of limitless growth propelled by globalization and free trade and everyone will be rich and content. Never mind the glaring inequities or the concentration of power. It's just a matter of time if we stay the course and don't let social or environmental "externalities" interfere with the free reign of the market. Eventually, everyone will prosper, all boats will rise. Peace is portrayed as economic subservience.

Global economic peace is bolstered by a none-too-subtle military preparedness to protect the centres of power. At the international and national levels, military resources are available and constantly being renewed so as to squelch serious threats to political or economic privilege. Peace is portrayed as dominance.

These are not the types of peace that Jesus brings. Jesus offers a peace that is simultaneously pragmatic and spiritual. His peace is infused with pragmatic justice and concerned with a Bangladeshi child's next meal, a pregnant Mexican woman's health in a *maquilladora* garment factory, the destruction of endangered old growth forests in Canada. His peace also provides a profound spiritual fulfilment. It is concerned with the nurturing of our relationships with God, with fellow human beings and with the natural world. Through such relationships, we experience the joy and satisfaction of loving and being loved. This is the abundant life that fulfils our spiritual needs.

Building just and sustainable communities based on peace as one of the spiritual values is a daunting task given the pervasiveness of violence in our contemporary societies. Engagement in struggles against the economic violence that impoverishes people and destroys much of the natural world is leading people of faith to challenge policies and practices from their local communities to the global level. Initiatives to build peace at the community level are involving churches in many parts of the world in playing a significant role in community efforts to reduce the level of domestic violence against women and children.

Addressing the violence in large urban areas is the focus of the Peace to the City campaign which grew out of the WCC's Programme to Overcome Violence, through which churches have been challenged to work together against systemic and personal violence. With a focus on seven cities, the campaign is highlighting creative models of peace-building and reconciled communities to make them visible, recognize the value of their approaches and methodologies, synthesize lessons learned to form new insights and theoretical perspectives, stimulate sharing and networking, and give others hope and the tools to attempt something similar in their own contexts. The seven cities participating in the campaign are Belfast, Northern Ireland; Boston, United States; Colombo, Sri Lanka; Durban, South Africa; Rio de Janeiro, Brazil; Suva, Fiji; and Kingston, Jamaica.

Creating conflict resolution alternatives that will reduce the potential for war is particularly urgent given the loss of life, destruction of communities and damage to the environment that armed conflict invariably entails. Fortunately, churches have considerable experience to contribute. During the 20th century, there were significant international ecumenical initiatives for peace, beginning with the efforts of the World Alliance for International Friendship through the Churches, continuing in the Life and Work Movement and later in the World Council of Churches, as well as many regional, national and later in local activities. In a speech to the 1994 Corrymeela consultation on "Nonviolent Approaches to Conflict Resolution", WCC general secretary Konrad Raiser summarized the ecumenical peace perspectives that had evolved out of the Justice, Peace and Integrity of Creation process:

1. War is no longer a legitimate means of interstate politics. Modern wars which are conducted with weapons of indiscriminate mass destruction have to be rejected and outlawed as a crime against humanity, using the ethical criteria of the just war doctrine.

2. Justice and peace are inseparably related. Peace is not only the absence of war, and the security of people is constantly threatened by conditions of structural injustice. Maintaining and building peace is a process which needs to be supported by the constant effort to broaden the reign of justice and the respect of human rights. The classical doctrine of the just war which aimed at the prevention or limitation of war has to be replaced today by the concept of a just peace. War can no longer be an act of justice.

3. Security is not only a military problem referring to the maintenance of order and the integrity of the state. What is at stake is the possibility of human life in security. Such security can only be maintained in cooperative ways as common security. Cooperative systems of security on a regional basis must, therefore, be considered as a decisive element in a new international order of peace.

4. The long-term witness of the historic peace churches for nonviolence receives new relevance in the present situation. It formulates the most basic challenge to the prevailing culture of violence and is, therefore, no longer a respectable but idealistic and apolitical position, but points towards the need to develop a new form of political reason which we have to learn if humanity is to survive.[4]

These observations illustrate the holistic approach in the ecumenical community that links peace to other fundamental values such as justice and love. Translating the values into action is not an easy task. Churches continue to be caught between their commitment to peace and their abhorrence of the brutality practised by repressive regimes, which seems to cry out for aggressive action to stop it. The war in Kosovo in 1999 was one such example. Though many people may have supported the NATO air strikes because of the ethnic cleansing being practised against Kosovar Albanians by the Milosevic government in Yugoslavia, most churches and ecumenical organizations did articulate policy positions that opposed the NATO strikes and emphasized the importance of pursuing nonviolent approaches to resolving the conflict. Citizen diplomacy is one such approach which I describe in the case study below.

The broadly-supported campaign against landmines is another example of an effort to translate the spiritual value of peace into practical action. Churches and church-sponsored peace groups were active members of the coalition which built public support sufficient to induce 122 governments to sign the Ottawa Landmines Treaty in December 1997. This coalition of non-governmental organizations won the Nobel Peace Prize. As successful as the campaign has been, the work is clearly not complete. Governments that have signed the treaty need to be monitored to ensure that they implement their commitments, and some major countries that still produce and use landmines – including the United States, Russia and China – have not yet agreed to the treaty and need to be pressured to do so.

Peace is a critical spiritual value for building sustainable communities in which all people and the broader natural world can thrive. Military, economic and personal violence does not have to dominate our societies unchallenged.

A case study: citizen diplomacy[5]

Translating the spiritual value of peace into a real-life foundation for just and sustainable communities is not an esoteric goal. Churches and ecumenical organizations provide leadership in developing new models to pursue peaceful resolutions to conflict situations ranging from domestic violence and community crime to national and international armed struggles.

In terms of international conflicts, faith groups and other non-governmental organizations have helped to build conditions for peace through development projects, human rights work and public witness for justice. An ecumenical peace coalition in Canada, Project Ploughshares, has developed considerable experience in training people for what is referred to as "citizen diplomacy", a model that is being implemented in various places around the world, particularly in conflict situations within countries.

Throughout much of the 20th century, the major source of armed conflict was war between countries. When disputes between states escalate, a variety of responses and entry points for conflict management are available to the international community – diplomatic missions, presidential hotlines, Security Council sessions, UN envoys, dispute settlement mechanisms in regional bodies like the Organization for African Unity or through international covenants and agreements, the use of third party good offices, and so on.

One of the dynamics in the world after the end of the cold war is the increase in conflicts *within* countries. In these cases, however, there does not seem to be the same range of resolution resources as for conflicts between countries. This is surprising, because state structures are generally regarded as far more developed than the international system in formal conflict management mechanisms. In the majority of states, to be sure, national political processes do work well enough to muddle through social and political conflicts and successfully avoid the resort to political violence. But the continuing high numbers of civil wars are tragic testimony to significant instances of the failure of state structures to work through serious political conflict and maintain both public order and confidence in the process.

Most diplomatic activity in the past has been focused through official government channels. This is sometimes referred to a "Track I Diplomacy". There is a continuing role for that approach, but its impact is limited if there is not broad support within communities for resolving conflicts and maintaining peace. A key element that has often been missing is a peace-building process and war prevention by middle-range leaders, such as people involved in ethnic, religious, humanitarian, cultural, educational, labour and academic organizations and sectors. This middle range is crucial in deepening a society's ability to resolve conflicts with justice, to address the psychological and social aspects of conflict, and to communicate between grassroots peace-building efforts and high-level negotiations.

In the absence of reliable and effective official-level response to local conflicts, the international NGO community has become much more active in exploring avenues of constructive, non-formal intervention. Non-governmental organizations, notably development and human rights agencies and religious communities, have long-standing and substantial links directly into many communities in conflict – a set of relationships that have not traditionally been seen as aids to diplomacy but which in the current circumstances of significant communal conflict are increasingly turned to for active peace-making.

But NGO involvement in peace-making tends not to be through negotiations among disputants. Civil wars born out of social chaos, communal rivalry and the failure of civil institutions to facilitate the peaceful settlement of internal disputes cannot be successfully mediated through negotiations by elites who no longer have the confidence of the people. The resolution of such conflicts in fact has much less to do with the settlement of particular disputes than with the restoration of relationships, of processes for social discourse and of institutions for collective decision-making that are fair and have the confidence of the people. It is the centrality of local communities to civil conflict that, on the one hand, impedes formal diplomatic intervention but, on the other, invites the informal interventions of non-governmental groups and civil society organizations. In a process focused on rebuilding relationships and public confidence, rather than on settling specific disputes, the fundamental requirement is to nurture a political culture of openness and inclusion – of participation in a public process that nurtures the public expectation that legitimate interests and grievances can and will be the subject of honest dialogue and accountable decision-making.

Citizen diplomacy came out of the cold-war period in the European efforts towards "détente from below" – that is, a citizens' movement to build links and cooperation on a people-to-people basis to challenge official enmity, to soften and transform public attitudes, and ultimately to change official behaviour and policy. The idea was based on the principle that human well-being requires security for all the people (common security) not just security of the state. Achieving and maintaining peace in societies could not just be left to governments but had to involve everyone in society. The march by Mothers of Russian Soldiers from Moscow to Grozny during the 1996 war on Chechnya was one example. There have been numerous citizen diplomacy initiatives by European churches to link with their counterparts in conflict regions in order to make a strong statement withholding moral legitimacy from the use of religion as a justification for war-making. The Conference of European Churches has put together various teams of religious leaders to visit and support their colleagues in Bosnia, Croatia, Kosovo and Serbia who are pressing for peaceful resolutions to tensions.

The concept of citizen diplomacy is evolving. Governments that recognize the need to draw on a wider set of societal resources than just their own diplomats are engaging other institutions such as universities, research institutes, peace groups. There is now use of what is referred to as "Track II Diplomacy" (or informal diplomacy) which is carried out or animated by citizens who do not have official roles but whose intention is directly to involve and engage officials and leaders in an informal process that is aimed at ultimately influencing official diplomacy. The original citizen diplomacy efforts did not involve government officials.

The International Resource Group on Disarmament and Security in the Horn of Africa (IRG), coordinated by the Canadian peace group Project Ploughshares, is one ongoing initiative in the Horn of Africa sub-region designed specifically to link an interested international civil society community to initiatives that support local civil society engagement in human and national security concerns. The IRG has elements of both citizen diplomacy and Track II Diplomacy. The context is an effort to engage civil society groups and individuals in exploring alternative approaches to security policy.

Of course, those creative, constructive alternatives emerge from the indigenous situation and civil society. Both the traditional structures and the new generations of professionals in Africa are as attuned to creative peace-building and conflict-management possibilities and methods as are their counterparts elsewhere, but they sometimes operate in political space that is heavily constrained – which means that a key objective of the IRG is to expand the political space for civil society groups in the Horn. The chosen mechanism in this instance is an international panel of prominent persons, primarily but not exclusively from Africa (non-Africans are included both for additional expertise and to assert international solidarity). Former and retired senior diplomats and military leaders, as well as internationally recognized experts and NGO leaders, form a panel to facilitate and host a process of indigenous research and informed public dialogue. The panel is designated the International Resource Group on Disarmament and Security in the Horn of Africa and functions at its core as an accompaniment programme. Standing with local civil society groups, its role is to confer legitimacy on indigenous research and analysis efforts, to interpret the research and analysis to political leaders, to invite government officials into the dialogue process, and generally to foster a climate of growing recognition that public engagement is a resource, not a threat, to good governance and effective conflict management.

The second priority is to promote a culture of openness and transparency to challenge prevailing assumptions (not only in the Horn but in most state security institutions) that secrecy is an aid to security (or at least preservation of the regime). Thus the IRG encourages the view that information is a public resource rather than the property of the elite. Public workshops and consultations are held at which representatives of the academic and research communities join NGOs and faith communities in multi-sectoral discussions of military/security issues based on publicly available information. In order to enhance this security discourse, the IRG assumes responsibility for mobilizing financial resources with which to commission new, locally based research.

The point is to enhance local research and analysis capacity and the knowledge base on which the slowly expanding public discourse can rely – in the process democratizing the security debate and mobilizing the public imagination towards new policy options. The policies applied by public officials, whether in democracies or in more restrictive societies, ultimately depend on a supply of credible policy options or alternatives. In other words, policy-makers ought to be able, in effect, to draw on a bank of publicly generated and tested available policy options. But, of course, it will be possible to make withdrawals from that policy options bank only if some deposits have been made. The point of democratizing the security debate and of engaging civil society in generating policy options is to enable societies to make regular deposits into the security policy options bank. When the political environment evolves and a new political will encourages it, timely withdrawals are possible.

Bethuel Kiplagat, a Kenyan diplomat who is involved in an IRG mediation project and has analyzed the impact of citizen diplomacy approaches in the Sudan, Uganda and Kenya, identifies the following lessons:

> We can affirm that the spirit of mediation is very much part of the African heritage. Unfortunately, due recognition has not being accorded to tested methods of conflict management.

In the three cases of Akobo, Wajir and Yei common threads emerge:

- There is explicit involvement of the community. The boundaries between the delegates and the community do not exist. Participation is by all – formally and informally.
- Music, dance, story-telling, and poetry play an important part as vehicles for conveying the peace message.
- The process is transparent, enabling the community and even passers-by to participate. There are no surprises.
- Note also the context. These are not bargaining sessions but healing processes – a re-establishment of relationship between people and also with their God. There is a holistic approach to the process, working with the community as a whole, invoking spiritual forces to be present and accompany the community towards peace.
- Whatever is agreed upon is seen as a blessing and a gift to be shared with the whole community. This came out most vividly in the cases of Akobo and Wajir. The peace-gift is owned by the community.
- The spiritual dimension weaves through the process – confession, forgiveness, reconciliation and the sealing of the peace covenant are dimensions which formal peace processes do not take into account.

After saying all that, maybe the time has come for those of us involved in conflict management and peace-building to go forward to "bush school" and humbly sit at the feet of the elders. Africa needs healing. We need to harness all our resources – traditional, intellectual and spiritual – for the building of peace in our troubled continent.[6]

NOTES

[1] Christopher Key Chapple, "Animals and Environment in the Buddhist Birth Stories", in Mary Evelyn Tucker and Duncan Ryuken Williams, eds, *Buddhism and Ecology: The Interconnection of Dharma and Deeds*, Harvard University Centre for the Study of World Religions, 1997, p.143.
[2] John Daido Loori, "The Precepts and the Environment", in *Buddhism and Ecology*.
[3] *Ibid.*, p.184.
[4] Konrad Raiser, "Peace on Earth: New Visions and New Praxis", address at the Corrymeela consultation on non-violent approaches to conflict resolution, June 1994, Geneva, WCC.

[5] I am indebted to Ernie Regehr of the Canadian peace group Project Ploughshares and Bonnie Greene of The United Church of Canada for valuable written and verbal input on citizen diplomacy. Material in this section is drawn primarily from Project Ploughshares resource entitled "International Resource Group Report – March 1999". Project Ploughshares can be contacted at the Institute of Peace and Conflict Studies, Conrad Grebel College, Waterloo, Ontario, Canada N2L 3G6; web site: www.ploughshares.ca. Additional useful material on citizen diplomacy in this case study was taken from a policy statement of the 35th general council of the United Church of Canada (Aug. 1994) entitled "Beyond Military Force: Seeking Peace after the Cold War".

[6] Bethuel Kiplagat, "Is Mediation Alien to Africa?", *Ploughshares Monitor*, Dec. 1998.

7. Faith and hope

> Now faith is the assurance of things hoped for, the conviction of things not seen. (Heb. 11:1)

What can sustain us to continue the struggle for just and sustainable communities in the face of our own fatigue and the overwhelming powers that seek to continue the oppression of so many in the human family and so much of the natural world?

Faith and hope.

The writer of the book of Hebrews in the New Testament defines faith as "the assurance of things hoped for, the conviction of things not seen". We hope for a time when no child will have to go to bed hungry. We hope for a world where children can play outside in the summer sun without their parents having to worry about sunscreen. We cannot as yet see minority communities free of toxic waste sites nor smaller countries able to sustain their economies unfettered by international trade restrictions. And yet, faith is the assurance and conviction that such a world of just and sustainable communities is possible.

Such faith seems almost impossible to us – a nearly insurmountable effort that we are compelled to make. But summoning such faith feels like a great burden only if we are starting from our own resources. We are weak and fragile beings in and of ourselves. Our vision is partial and our energy is limited. Our best efforts at working for ecological sustainability and social justice seem inadequate to the task and the strength of the forces mounted against us.

But the faith described by the writer of Hebrews does not originate with us. Our faith is a response to the covenantal relationship that God has initiated with all the creation. We can have faith in God because we know that God loves us.

We can have faith:

- that God seeks a world where humans live in relationships of peace and justice with each other and with the natural world;
- that we are able, with God's help, to discern what we should do to participate in ushering God's shalom; and
- that God loves us and will remain with us in the struggles.

The faith of Abraham and Sarah in the Old Testament illustrates the seemingly incomprehensible and responsive nature of faith. Abraham did not believe that God could make him father of a great nation when he was already so old. Sarah, his wife, found it incredible that she could bear a child at her advanced age. The possibilities of these "things hoped for" seemed so remote that both Abraham and Sarah laughed at the prospect. But God promised that it would happen. In response to God's promise and the covenant that God established with them, Abraham and Sarah believed. They had faith in God and God's promise and it came about.

It is not easy to summon this faith when the obstacles seem so great. But one of the wonderful and ironic things about faith is that we are most likely to attain it by not trying so hard. When we recognize our total dependence on God, when we can let the burden of the world's woes slip from our shoulders and share it with God, when we can come to God in prayer, then faith blooms.

C.S. Lewis had an interesting way of describing the relationship between our best efforts to live as responsibly as possible and our dependence on God.

A serious moral effort is the only thing that will bring you to the point where you throw up the sponge [i.e. recognize that your own efforts are inadequate]. Faith in Christ is the only thing to save you from despair at that point: and out of that faith in him good actions must inevitably come.[1]

As Lewis notes, the relationship between faith and works is cyclical or synergistic. Our own efforts and our own strength will always be inadequate to the magnitude of the task. We need faith in God that reassures us that we are not alone and that what we are about is what God would have us be about. But we cannot just leave it to God. We will not appreciate the depth of our need for faith without the intense personal engagement in working for justice, peace and the integrity of creation. Our faith in God becomes real when we are engaged in God's real work. That faith then re-energizes us for further engagement. We have no choice. Faith in God compels us to commit ourselves to work for earth community. It is a commitment which we accept not with resignation but with a deep sense of spiritual satisfaction.

The relationship between faith and works has often been a troubling one and not only for Christian believers. Some of the early conflicts within Islam centred around the debate as to whether faith was sufficient to assure one of being reconciled with God at the time of judgment or whether it required righteous works. As has been the case with theological polarizations in various religions, schools of thought emerged to reconcile the two.[2]

Faith is a critical element in many of Jesus' miracles. Jesus heals the son of the centurion because Jesus is so impressed with the centurion's faith (Matt. 8:5-13). Jesus tells the hemorrhaging woman that it is her faith that has made her well (Matt. 9:20-22). These miracles illumine a different angle from which to appreciate the gifts that faith can bring. Not only does faith give us the energy to be engaged in daunting struggles for earth community, but it can also be the reason we receive that for which we hope and pray. The faith of the centurion and of the woman was what Jesus credited as the basis for the miracle. There is an important distinction to note here. They did not have faith in order to be assured of the healing. Faith does not lend itself to utilitarian manipulation in order for us to get what we want. Rather, the miracles occurred because they had faith. Our free and unconditional surrender in faith can yield this bounty in response.

Faith provides a security in our commitment but it would be a dry commitment without hope. Hope adds the additional element of joy, expectation, excitement, celebration. Hope gives us the energy to continue our struggles and to be able to sing along the way.

Hope is a difficult spiritual gift to describe. It is much more than a glib optimism that everything will turn out fine, because in fact we do not know that everything will turn out fine. Neither is hope an intentional ignoring of the serious problems that confront the world and the obstacles to sustainable living. Hope takes seriously those realities but refuses to be drowned by them.

The WCC study document, *Climate Change and the Quest for Sustainable Societies,* concludes with an interesting reflection on hope. Certainly, climate change – in its magnitude and the implications of efforts to address it – has to be one of the most overwhelming challenges that humanity has ever had to face. Can there be hope when confronted with such a threat?

> Christian hope has often been individual and tribal: hope for one's own redemption and for one's nearest and dearest. It has also been a "shalom" vision oriented to another world, one inhabited only by Christians. Our conversion to the earth (who we are) and our calling to work for the well-being of the entire household (what we must do), means that our hope changes as well. We do not hope just for eternal life in another world, but for a transformed life in this world. We hope for the kindom's[3] well-being.

> But what sort of hope are we justified in maintaining? There is a very deep conviction in Western thought that human history is characterized by the march of progress. This belief has both infected and been reinforced by Christian theology. A document from the 1961 assembly of the WCC states that "the Christian should welcome scientific discoveries as new steps in man's

domination of nature".[4] The pastoral constitution *Gaudium et Spes* of the Second Vatican Council expressed a general expectation that "... (human beings), created in God's image, received a mandate to subject (to themselves) the earth and all that it contains... thus, by the subjugation of all things to (humanity), the name of God would be wonderful in all the earth."[5]

From this viewpoint, it was the duty of the churches to follow this movement critically but above all constructively. Obstacles and even setbacks were to be expected. Nevertheless, Christians could start from the certainty that God would lead humanity over all the obstacles to the historical fulfilment God had intended. To be sure, God's kingdom lay beyond any kind of fulfilment within human history. But there was a connection between the ongoing course of history and ultimate fulfilment in the kingdom of God, for the forces of the kingdom were already at work in the history of humankind.

These considerations lead almost inevitably to the conclusion that human history will be "sustainable" in all circumstances. They supply the motivation for a critical militancy. They do not, however, take into account the possibility that the historical project to which humanity has been committed for decades can, as such, bear within itself the seeds of self-destruction. Accordingly, on the basis of these perspectives, it was difficult to make out the crisis at an early stage, for surely that would have called into question the achievements which we have celebrated as human progress for so many years.

The current hopes for the future, therefore, increasingly show themselves to be quite illusory. The ecological crisis makes us aware that self-destruction is a real possibility to be reckoned with. For theology to downplay the signs which point in this direction would be to turn itself into ideology. The only appropriate understanding of hope is one which integrates the signs of decay. The future is radically open. Hope which takes reality into account has to face the possibility of the failure and even the end of the human race. That does not mean that all hope must be abandoned. But real hope must rely on the conviction that the future is ultimately in God's hands – "for yours is the kingdom", as we say each time we recite the Lord's prayer.

This does not mean surrendering to fatalism. The hope that ultimately all is in God's hands is a source of freedom. Precisely because it liberates us from the compulsion of the ideologies of growth and progress, it enables us to accept the challenge and to strike out on paths that at first sight look like steps backwards. Those who make their behaviour dependent on growth and success will soon be discouraged. The expectation of God's kingdom of love makes us capable of love even irrespective of the course finally taken by history. From one moment to the next, we shall stand up for the preservation of God's gift of life. What is involved here is something like an Hippocratic oath uniting the churches and to which they must be committed in view of the phenomena of disintegration and decay. It is a matter of opposing the destruction of life with commitment and forethought.[6]

Hope is one of the very important contributions which faith communities can make to the broader movements for social change and ecological protection. Because the problems often seem so overwhelming, people can easily become discouraged. Religious communities can offer deeper spiritual resources such as hope to help sustain the efforts of the many others around the world who share our commitment to peace, justice and the protection of creation.

In my work on earth community issues both for the United Church of Canada and for the WCC, I have considerable involvement with people from UN agencies, non-governmental organizations, governments, business and industry. As churches, ecumenical organizations and faith groups, we are relatively small players in these engagements whether at the level of international negotiations or a local environmental conflict. But time and again, people tell me how much they appreciate the participation of faith groups because they say that we bring a spiritual perspective and a source of hope which is sorely needed. They confide this to me quietly, because they acknowledge that in our increasingly secularized societies, discussion of values and spirituality is highly suspect. They lament that they cannot explicitly articulate such perspectives in their secular capacity even though they have their own faith convictions. But they are convinced that the problems that we are facing in trying to foster sustainable communities go far beyond economics, science and politics. They tell me repeatedly that they recognize that the obstacles are profoundly ethical in nature and the long-term solutions require a rediscovery of spirituality. In their mind, faith groups bring those perspectives and hence give them a sense of hope.

The nurturing of faith and the sustaining of hope is not easily accomplished in isolation. It is in community that we learn and grow. Faith communities can open us to new ideas of what the Spirit of God may be calling us to in this day and age. Within faith communities, we can experience fundamental values and dynamic ethical criteria to help us analyze the world around us. Through faith communities, we can build supportive networks to challenge consumerism, economic globalization, and violence and to model new ways of just and sustainable living.

Larry Rasmussen's book *Moral Fragments, Moral Community* explores the ways in which contemporary Western societies undermine the formation of community and the roles that collective groups, churches in particular, can play in facilitating the moral development needed to address the social and ecological challenges facing us. This need not be intimidating:

> What we are seeking is crucial but infinitely more modest; namely, that kind of gracious domain in which, amid caring for others and they for us, we learn the art of understanding the moral positions of others so indispensable to public life itself. Most of these communities are voluntary, they affirm individual dignity without enshrining individualism and they generate authority. But it is authority that members themselves generate, to which they consent, and for which they themselves are accountable.[7]

Rasmussen illustrates this in a discussion of the role of practices within faith communities. "So very often the moral soundness of the world beyond the church is served best by faith communities that live out that moral soundness in the detail of their own ranks."[8] The objective of fostering just and sustainable communities provides such an opportunity to churches. Several years ago, we produced a poster in our denomination entitled "Make Your Church a Creation-Awareness Centre".[9] It listed ideas, some ambitious but most modest, for ways in which congregations could reflect their commitment to care and justice for all God's creatures through the educational, liturgical, outreach and operational aspects of the church's life.

Faith and hope are possible when we recognize that we are not alone. Indeed, we are not alone – we live in God's world and can be supported within faith communities.

A case study: gardening

I am not a sophisticated gardener. I am probably not even a good gardener. But gardening brings faith and hope alive for me. I am not alone. Gardeners around the world depend on this potent combination of faith and hope. Many people and their families survive on the grains, fruit and vegetables that they coax from the soil. Such gardens are not grown for the beauty they produce but for their life-sustaining nourishment. Others have little plots in a community garden, a flower box on their balcony, or a few pots on their window-ledge. Regardless of the purpose, the miracle of plant growth is still the same. New life is created, over and over again, year after year.

As I sit at my desk writing these words, I can look out the window at the side garden. It is August in Canada and the sun is shining brilliantly on some deep purple delphiniums, white caltonias and red geraniums. The colours stand out all the more because of the background of rich green provided by the cedar hedge behind them.

Though I know a bit about botany and the ecological sciences, I do not really comprehend how the flowers in our garden issue forth from inconsequential seeds, the ragged-looking stubble left from the previous year's growth, or little cuttings bought at the local farmers' market. All I know is that with care and tending and the blessings of sun and rain, the flowers will appear. I have faith that they will come and when that faith is rewarded, my hope in life for today and for tomorrow is rejuvenated.

There is a peacefulness in gardening. I feel as if I'm meditating when I have my hands in the soil or when I'm sitting on the grass weeding out the dandelions and creeping charlie.

A walk around our modest garden prompts a few reflections. I stop at the two clematis plants on either side of the back door. On the left, the trellis is no longer visible because of the profusion of growth of small dark green leaves and the residue of early summer blossoms. There is no difficulty in seeing the trellis on the right – a single slender stock struggles to maintain its few remaining leaves. Here are two similar plants growing under similar conditions and yet with dramatically different results – the unpredictability of life. Though we can and must do our best to live responsible individual and collective lives, we cannot be certain of the outcome. Even the transformative power of spiritual values as a foundation for life does not assure us of being able to realize just and sustainable communities. We must use our capacities of discernment to follow God's call as best we can. But ultimately, we have no guarantee of the outcome. What we do know is that we are not alone – we are in God's hands.

Around the corner is the knot garden,[10] a small plot where foot-high boxwood shrubs planted closely together and pruned over several years now form the outline of the Christian symbol of a fish, the Greek first letter of Christ's name. Viewed from the end, it appears to be a ribbon. My partner and I planted it to have the dual significance of a botanical witness to our Christian faith and to represent an AIDS ribbon. This little section of our garden serves as a memorial plot with a few rose bushes in the middle interspersed with small plaques holding the names of friends who have died of AIDS. Gardens are poignant illustrations of the cycles of life in which death figures prominently. Accepting the harsh and inevitable reality of death is perhaps the ultimate test of our faith in a loving God and our hope for the renewal of life.

Finally, near the kitchen door, I pause at a wooden frame about four feet by eight feet with posts rising at each of the corners and holding soil about two feet deep. This is our four-poster vegetable bed. The growth here does not nourish the soul with its beauty as the flowers do, yet the vegetables provide sustenance for our bodies. We are all dependent on the miracle of growth to fill our most basic needs. Many of us living in urban centres may not come into contact with the physical process – produce seems to appear magically on the grocer's shelves. Whether we are conscious of it or not, the food we eat comes to our table as the result of human labour. We experience here again the inextricable connection between the integrity of creation and justice within the human community for any discussion of agriculture today must acknowledge the many challenges and complexities:

- organic farmers trying to make the transition away from agriculture dependent on the intense use of chemical fertilizers and pesticides;
- small family farms struggling to survive amidst the burgeoning influence of agribusiness and international agricultural trade policy;
- peasants fighting for land reform to gain access to huge tracts of land currently the private reserve of the privileged few, while the poor need the small plots to grow food for their families;
- valuable agricultural land threatened by human-induced climate change through droughts in areas of large landmass, rainfall occurring in more extreme events causing flooding, and rising sea levels inundating fertile delta regions;
- the biotechnology industry exporting its genetically modified seeds with the promise of feeding the hungry while ensuring a greater dependence of the farmer on these transnational companies.

Our little vegetable garden connects me to that broader world. The growth of food is dependent on the health of God's creation and on the socio-economic well-being of the human community. The local and the global are linked.

I am reminded that we are not alone – we live in God's world. With each new season of growth in the garden, my faith is renewed and my hope confirmed.

Thanks be to God.

124

NOTES

[1] C.S. Lewis, *Mere Christianity*, Glasgow, Scotland, Collins, 1952, pp.127-28.
[2] See H.A.R. Gibb, "Islam", in R.C. Zaehner, ed., *The Concise Encyclopedia of Living Faiths*, Boston, Beacon Press, 1967, p.190.
[3] "Kindom", referring to an understanding of God's household as containing all God's creatures i.e. all the "kin", is discussed earlier in the WCC study document from which this quote is taken.
[4] Wesley Granberg-Michaelson, "Creation in Ecumenical Theology", in David G. Hallman, ed., *Ecotheology: Voices from South and North*, Geneva, WCC, and Maryknoll, NY, Orbis, 1994, p.97.
[5] *Gaudium et Spes*, Second Vatican Council, p.34.
[6] WCC, "Climate Change and the Quest for Sustainable Societies", Geneva, WCC, 1998, pp.40-41. The study document was prepared after a consultation involving participants from around the world. The theological reflections which form the last chapter and these paragraphs on hope in particular were drafted primarily by theologians Sallie McFague and Lukas Vischer.
[7] Larry Rasmussen, *Moral Fragments, Moral Community*, Minneapolis, Fortress Press, 1993, pp.132-33.
[8] *Ibid.*, p.153.
[9] United Church of Canada, "Make Your Church a Creation-Awareness Centre", Toronto, UCC, 1996.
[10] A "knot garden" is a Middle English term referring to "a design or figure formed of crossing lines... a flower-bed laid out in an intricate design" (Oxford English Dictionary).

4. Suggestions for Group Study

The following are three possible models for organizing group study using *Spiritual Values for Earth Community* as a resource.

1. Study programme with one session

If the group has one session in which to discuss the book, it will not be possible to get into a detailed analysis of each chapter. Chapter 3 would be the most important section on which to focus, with an initial brief discussion of Chapter 2. If all members of the group have had an opportunity to read the book, then members could break up into small groups for discussion after a brief introduction. If only the leader has access to the book, then a brief summary will be required.

- Welcoming, introductions, worship
- Brief summary of the main arguments of the book
  - Values play an important role in the decisions we make about our individual lives and the ways we organize our communities and societies.
  - The values that dominate in many societies currently are consumerism, economic globalization and violence. These values are resulting in an increasing marginalization of the poor, social injustice, and destruction of the environment.
  - Spiritual values could help us build more just and sustainable communities if we incorporated them more fully into our own lives and the ways that we organize ourselves collectively. The spiritual values described in the book in terms of their implications for just and sustainable living are gratitude, humility, sufficiency, justice, peace, love, faith and hope.
- Plenary discussion in response to the question: What do you see as the predominant values influencing our community and society?
- Break into small groups to discuss the following questions:
  - What do you think would be the differences in our community and society if greater emphasis were placed on spiritual values?

- – Which spiritual values do you think are the most important in working towards just and sustainable communities?
- – Are there spiritual values other than those discussed in this book which you think are important to emphasize?
- Plenary discussion to hear and discuss responses from small groups
- Closing

2. Study programme with two sessions

If the group has the opportunity to meet twice to discuss issues arising from the book, then the first session could be spent on general introduction and overview with a concentration on Chapters 1 and 2 and the second session could focus on Chapter 3. If all members of the group have had an opportunity to read the book, then one could move into the small-group discussion period after a brief introduction. If only the leader has access to the book, then a brief summary will be required.

First session
- Welcoming, introductions, worship
- Brief summary of the main arguments of the book
- Small-group discussion focused on Chapter 1: What role do you think values play in the decisions we make about our own life-styles and in the way that we organize our communities and societies?
- Plenary discussion to hear and discuss responses from small groups.
- Small-group discussion focused on Chapter 2: What do you see as the predominant values influencing our community and society?
- Plenary discussion to hear and discuss responses from small groups
- Closing

Second session
- Welcoming, introductions, worship
- Plenary discussion on the role of spiritual values: What do you think would be the differences in our community

and society if greater emphasis were placed on spiritual values?

- Small-group discussion concentrating on Chapter 3:
  - Which spiritual values do you think are the most important in working towards just and sustainable communities?
  - Are there spiritual values other than those discussed in this book that you think are important to emphasize?
  - What steps could we take in our own lives and community that would build on spiritual values and lead to more justice and environmental protection?
- Plenary discussion to hear and discuss responses from small groups

3. Study programme with multiple sessions

If the group has the opportunity to meet on several occasions, a more detailed study process can be organized. In addition to following the general outline listed above, more in-depth sessions could be held on the implications of specific spiritual values, with an accompanying related Bible study. Sessions could also include project planning for action that the group might want to take to implement some of their ideas in working towards just and sustainable communities.

If all members of the group have had an opportunity to read the book, then one could move into the small group discussion period after a brief introduction. If only the leader has access to the book, then a brief summary will be required.

First session
- Welcoming, introductions, worship
- Brief summary of the main arguments of the book
- Small-group discussion focused on Chapter 1: What role do you think values play in the decisions we make about our own life-styles and in the way we organize our communities and societies?
- Plenary discussion to hear and discuss responses from small groups

128

- Small-group discussion focused on Chapter 2: What do you see as the predominant values influencing our community and society?
- Plenary discussion to hear and discuss responses from small groups
- Closing

Second session
- Welcoming, introductions, worship
- Plenary discussion on the role of spiritual values: What do you think would be the differences in our community and society if greater emphasis were placed on spiritual values?
- Small-group discussion concentrating on Chapter 3:
  - Which spiritual values do you think are the most important in working towards just and sustainable communities?
  - Are there spiritual values other than those discussed in this book that you think are important to emphasize?
  - What spiritual values or clusters of values would you like to focus on in greater detail in subsequent sessions?
- Plenary discussion to hear and discuss responses from small groups

Subsequent sessions
- Welcoming, introductions, worship
- Plenary discussion and Bible study on a specific spiritual value or cluster of values (Bible study ideas can be found in each of the sub-sections in Chapter 3)
- Small-group discussion on the specific spiritual value or cluster of values which are the focus of that session:
  - What steps could we take in our own lives and community that would build on this (these) spiritual value(s) and lead to more justice and environmental protection?
  - What are the obstacles that need to be overcome?

- – What partners in the community and other sources of support could we work with?
- Plenary discussions to hear and discuss responses from small groups

Appendix: Further Reading

There are an increasing number of useful books that explore the challenges of working towards just and sustainable communities. The following short list is by no means comprehensive but reflects some of the recent publications that I have found helpful.

Body of God: An Ecological Theology, by Sallie McFague, Augsburg Fortress Press, 1993.

Buddhism and Ecology, ed. by Mary Evelyn Tucker and Duncan Ryuken Williams, Harvard University Centre for the Study of World Religions, 1997.

Christianity and Ecology: Seeking the Well-being of Earth and Humans, ed. by Dieter T. Hessel and Rosemary Radford Ruether, Harvard University Centre for the Study of World Religions, 2000.

The Consuming Passion: Christianity and the Consumer Culture, ed. by Rodney Clapp, Inter-Varsity Press, 1998.

Cry of the Earth, Cry of the Poor, by Leonardo Boff, Orbis Books, 1997.

Earth Community, Earth Ethics, by Larry Rasmussen, Orbis Books, 1996.

The Ecology of Commerce, by Paul Hawken, Harper Business Books, 1993.

Ecotheology: Voices from South and North, ed. by David G. Hallman, WCC Publications and Orbis Books, 1994.

Factor Four: Doubling Wealth – Halving Resource Use, by Amory and Hunter Lovins and Ernst von Weizsäcker, Earthscan Books, 1996.

For the Common Good: Redirecting the Economy Toward Community, the Environment and a Sustainable Future, by Herman Daly and John Cobb Jr., Beacon Press, 1989.

Gaia and God: An Ecofeminist Theology of Earth Healing, by Rosemary Radford Ruether, Harper San Francisco Books, 1992.

How Much Is Enough? The Consumer Society and the Future of the Earth, by Alan Durning, W.W. Norton Publishers, 1992.

Moral Fragments, Moral Community, by Larry Rasmussen, Fortress Press, 1993.

Our Common Future, World Commission on Environment and Development, Oxford UP, 1987.

A Place in Creation: Visions in Science, Religion and Economics, by David G. Hallman, United Church of Canada Publishing House, 1992.

Simplicity: Notes, Stories and Exercises for Developing Unimaginable Wealth, by Mark A. Burch, New Society Publishers, 1995.

Theology for Earth Community, ed. by Dieter Hessel, Orbis Books, 1996.

Vital Signs, by Lester Brown et al, W.W. Norton Publishers, 1999.

Wisdom of the Elders, by Peter Knudtson and David Suzuki, Stoddart Publishing, 1992.

Risk
BOOK SERIES

The Risk Book Series from WCC Publications deals with issues of crucial importance to Christians around the world today. Each volume contains well-informed and provocative perspectives on current concerns in the ecumenical movement, written in an easy-to-read style for a general church audience.

Although any Risk book may be ordered separately, those who subscribe to the series are assured of receiving all four volumes published during the year by airmail immediately upon publication – at a substantial savings on the price for individual copies. In addition to the four new titles each year, occasional "Risk Specials" are published. Although subscribers are not automatically sent these books as part of their subscription, they are notified of their appearance and invited to purchase them under the same advantageous conditions.

If you wish to subscribe to the Risk series, please send your name and address to WCC Publications, P.O. Box 2100, 1211 Geneva 2, Switzerland. Details and an order form will be sent to you by return mail.

Some of the titles published recently in the Risk Book Series are:

Bas de Gaay Fortman and Berma Klein Goldewijk
Where Needs Meet Rights
Economic, Social and Cultural Rights in a New Perspective

The poverty, violence and globalization which are depriving more and more people of basic human entitlements – food, housing, livelihood and health – call for creative new approaches to economic and social rights which, the authors say, must be rooted in human needs, human dignity and legitimacy and undergirded by religious convictions. 160pp.

Andrew Wingate
Does Theological Education Make a Difference?
Global Lessons in Mission and Ministry
from India and Britain
The importance of doing and learning theology in a way that is authentic to each particular cultural situation in which the gospel is proclaimed is widely acknowledged. But what difference does radically contextual theological education make once the student begins ministry in the parish? 126pp.

Gillian Paterson
Still Flowing
Women, God and Church
The author reflects on the key questions that face women and men in the churches today, drawing on the lessons of the Ecumenical Decade – Churches in Solidarity with Women. A series of seven "Windows" select biblical stories relating to the issues discussed and offer an imaginative retelling of them from the point of view of the (usually silent) women actors in them. 142pp.

S. Wesley Ariarajah
Not Without My Neighbour
Issues in Interfaith Relations
Drawing on his wide experience, the author deals with key concerns that arise out of the experience of inter-religious encounter and dialogue: interfaith worship, marriage across religious lines, the search for a "global ethic" and education for life in a multifaith society. 138pp.

Dafne Plou
Peace in Troubled Cities
Creative Models of Building Community amidst Violence
This book recounts stories of creative community engagement to rebuild community out of situations of alienation, violence and hopelessness, emerging from the seven cities in the WCC's "Peace to the City" campaign: Belfast, Boston, Colombo, Kingston, Durban, Rio de Janeiro and Suva. 140pp.

134

John Pobee and Gabriel Ositelu II
African Initiatives in Christianity
The Growth, Gifts and Diversities of Indigenous African Churches – a Challenge to the Ecumenical Movement
Much of the rapid growth of Christianity in Africa is occurring in the African Independent (or Indigenous) Churches (AICs), founded by Africans for Africans and expressing their faith in genuinely African cultural forms and styles. Two African theologians and church leaders – one from an historic church, one from an AIC – examine what this implies for the future of the ecumenical movement. 88pp

Margot Kaessmann
Overcoming Violence
The Challenge to the Churches in All Places
What can churches do together effectively to overcome violence in the home, on the streets, in the media? What resources for nonviolent resolution of conflicts can they find in the Bible and their theological traditions? 96pp.

Rob van Drimmelen
Faith in a Global Economy
A Primer for Christians
Lucid explanations of the major ideas, forces and realities of the world economy today: globalization, international trade, transnational corporations, international finance, employment and unemployment, land and resources, markets and growth. 170pp.